CONSTRUCTION IN PROGRESS

Building a better Christian, one project at a time

by Hal Hammons

2013 One Stone Press.
All rights reserved. No part of this book may be reproduced
in any form without written permission of the publisher.

Scripture taken from the NEW AMERICAN STANDARD BIBLE®,
©1960, 1962, 1963, 1968, 1971, 1972, 1973, 1975, 1977, 1995
by The Lockman Foundation. Used by permission.

Published by:
One Stone Press
979 Lovers Lane
Bowling Green, KY 42103

Printed in the United States of America

ISBN 10: 0-985-4938-3-6
ISBN 13: 978-0-985-4938-3-7

Supplemental Materials Available:
PowerPoint slides for each lesson
Answer key
Downloadable PDF

www.onestone.com

INTRODUCTION

"Therefore, putting aside all malice and all deceit and hypocrisy and envy and all slander, like newborn babies, long for the pure milk of the word, so that by it you may grow in respect to salvation, if you have tasted the kindness of the Lord."
—1 Peter 2:1-3

Meet Adam. Adam learned the truth about Jesus Christ from his own study and from studying with his friends in the church. He had always had a vague notion of God but had not been regular in any sort of religious practice. A few weeks ago he realized the error of his ways and his need for a real relationship with Jesus Christ. And so he made Jesus His Lord, putting him on in baptism as his friends rejoiced.

Meet Brooke. Brooke's background is very different from Adam's, having been reared by godly parents and going to worship services all her life. As she grew in years, she grew in faith as well, gradually understanding more and more about sin and obedience. Finally, she reached the "age of accountability" the preacher was always talking about, and she acted on her faith.

Meet Clyde. Clyde has been a Christian for decades. He has been a stalwart member of his home congregation, leading prayers, reading Scripture publicly, doing the best he could do as his body gradually began to fail. He led singing from time to time in his youth, even trying his hand at the occasional short devotional talk. But he now sees his life as a Christian more in the past tense than in the future tense.

All three of these Christians have something in common—the need to grow. They will develop at different speeds, and the result of their development will be different. But they all grow in the same direction—toward the example of Jesus Christ. This is a process that began at the point of their spiritual birth and will—or at least, should—continue to the day they pass from this life into the next.

All parents want their children to grow, to achieve, and to become bigger and better in the tasks set before them. Our heavenly Father is no different with regard to His spiritual children. He has begotten us in Christ (1 John 5:1), and that is an excellent start. But His work in us is not complete when we submit to baptism in the name of Jesus; it has only begun. We must continue to work out our salvation (Philippians 2:12).

This book is intended to help the child of God do exactly that.

We often think of coming to Christ as an exercise in self-denial—don't do this, don't do that, etc. And certainly that is a vital part of our walk with Christ. But the main reason we get rid of the worldliness in our heart is so there will be room in it for Jesus. And the more we rid ourselves of the impurities that would hinder our development, the more we will be in position for the gospel to do its work in us, to have its way with us.

The transformation Jesus is working in us is a demonstration of His kindness, as Peter indicates. It may not always seem kind at the moment, but in truth the best and most loving thing Jesus can do for us is to rid us of "the sin which so easily entangles us" (Hebrews 12:1), and give us profitable, noble, spiritual labor to replace it. This should be the very epitome of a "labor of love." Yes, it is work. But we love the work. We are challenged by the barriers we erect between ourselves and the Lord—but not daunted, not immobilized. With God's help, we know we can be up to any challenge. And when we prove to be less than worthy on a particular occasion, we accept the forgiveness that is in Jesus, dust ourselves off, and commit ourselves to better effort in the future.

Some might be put off by the prospect of always striving for perfection, yet never achieving it. But that attitude, frankly, is rooted in laziness. God did not give us a task to achieve, as though He would be done with us after we had done so; He gave us a mark to strive for—the example of His own Son (1 Peter 2:21). Like a runner who always knows his best time has not yet been attained, like a weightlifter who knows he can get even stronger if he will work even harder, so the Christian has confidence that there is always room for growth. And unlike the physical examples given, we are not limited by external factors such as age and health. No matter how long we may remain here on earth, we can serve our Lord even better every day than we did the day before if we will only commit ourselves to the task. After all, the power is not in us. It never was. It is in Him and His gospel.

May He give the increase, both in us and in others.

NOTES FOR TEACHERS

This book is designed to help a Christian grow, regardless of the context. But it is especially written with a class environment in mind. Given that most churches have weekly or biweekly classes of 45 minutes or so apiece, 12 per quarter, I wrote the book around those parameters.

My suggestion for class organization is this: take two class periods per lesson, with each period divided roughly into three blocks.

- **Block 1a:** Summarize the introduction, "Where we start," and "How we grow" sections of the lesson.

- **Block 1b:** Review class answers to the discussion questions. Emphasize the particular struggle that new converts, young people and the elderly have with regard to spiritual growth.

- **Block 1c:** Compare answers to the "prayer" construction zone. Have a designated man take notes of everyone's responses to the prompts and compose a prayer to lead for the group. He should feel free to use the introductory sentences provided or compose his own. But the prayer should specifically target the lesson topic and incorporate most or all of the class members' input.

- **Block 2a:** Have a designated man choose a song relating to the lesson topic, take a few moments to explain why he chose that particular song, and lead it. Follow up with a discussion of the "worship" construction zone.

- **Block 2b:** Summarize the "The 'finished' product" section of the lesson. Emphasize that there is always improvement to be made in our growth.

- **Block 2c:** Discuss the "evangelism" construction zone. Spur conversation regarding how we can use the lesson to reach lost souls.

My hope and prayer is that you will be able to foster growth in yourself and others with this material as much as I have grown in its development. God bless.

Hal Hammons
Pace, Florida
July 2013

TABLE OF CONTENTS

1. Building Faith 9

2. Building Trust 15

3. Building Hope 21

4. Building Love 27

5. Building Desire 33

6. Building Patience 39

7. Building Walls 45

8. Building Enthusiasm 51

9. Building Confidence 57

10. Building Relationships 63

11. Building Bridges 69

12. Building Joy 75

LESSON 1

BUILDING FAITH

Sometimes words are not necessary.

Such was the case for a young man who was sorely afflicted with an embarrassing, debilitating, and potentially fatal affliction. He could not tell his father how much he was suffering, but his father knew. Everyone knew. How could they not know?

And so the father brought him to Jesus. Desperately clinging to any semblance of hope, he cried out to the Lord, "But if You can do anything, take pity on us and help us!"

Jesus was compassionate. But even so, He could not help but remark on the man's shaky faith. Certainly his recent disappointment (Jesus' disciples had utterly failed to cure his son) had left him doubting even God's power to save. But even though his faith was not what it could have been, or should have been, he had enough to know where faith could be found.

"I do believe; help my unbelief."

I often find myself thinking of the story told in Mark 9:14-29, and especially the father's plaintive cry in verse 24. I am a believer. I have never stopped believing. But surely a believer would not be struggling with doubt like this. Help my unbelief, Lord. Help my unbelief.

We all have a demon or two (or several) with whom we do spiritual battle. Maybe it's alcohol. Maybe it's materialism. Maybe it's homosexuality. Sometimes we win; far too often we lose. But hopefully, like the boy's father, we have enough faith to recognize the weakness of our faith. And we remember the origin of our faith—the divine word of God (Romans 10:17), a demonstration of the Spirit of truth sent from Jesus Christ Himself (John 16:13). We, desperate, reach out to Him again. And He, merciful, agrees to "perfect, confirm, strengthen and establish" the weak of spirit (1 Peter 5:10).

Where we start

Like many of my readers, I came to faith gradually. My parents were Christians. My grandparents were Christians. There probably has not been a single handful of Sundays in my life when I was either in church services or prohibited from doing so by reason of health. I learned who made the world when I was 1, who built the ark when

I was 2, and who climbed the sycamore tree when I was 3. And the whole time, I was also learning that Jesus died for my sins. I didn't understand it fully when I was 3—but then, I don't understand it fully now. Eventually I realized I had to act on my faith, such as it was, and so at the age of 10 I was baptized. It has been a long journey, with many steps forward and several steps backward. But now, almost four decades later, I can look back and see how my faith progressed.

Having children has allowed me to relive the experience again. My second daughter, Kylie, watched at the tender age of 8 as her sister, Taylor, was baptized. Being especially focused on spiritual things even then, she immediately began asking Tracie and me when would be the right time for her to be baptized. Through one study after another, through one prayer after another, she kept asking. And all we could think to tell her was, "When the time is right, you will know." I don't know if that was the best or most eloquent thing we could have said, but I suppose it worked. A couple of years later she quit asking if the time was right and started telling us the time was right. She took control of her own faith instead of trying to mimic that of her sister or her parents.

Adam says:

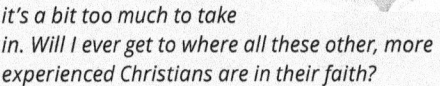

I believed in Jesus enough to be baptized. But I'm not sure what else I believe. A lot of the Bible seems like it's a bit too much to take in. Will I ever get to where all these other, more experienced Christians are in their faith?

However you came in contact with Jesus, either gradually or suddenly, you had one of those moments as well—the moment when you say to yourself, "I believe in Jesus. And Jesus wants me to be baptized. I don't want to wait any longer. I can't wait any longer." And on that day, when you decide to trade your conceptual faith for an obedient faith, you became a Christian.

This is the "one faith" of Ephesians 4:5. It gives substance to our hopes and aspirations (Hebrews 11:1). It brings us into contact with the saving grace of God (Ephesians 2:8). It makes us different from unbelievers and motivates us to separate ourselves even more (Galatians 2:20). Peter's confession of Jesus was the bedrock foundation upon which the entire church was founded (Matthew 16:18), and it serves as the foundation for our own personal relationship with God as well (1 Corinthians 3:11).

How we grow

There is a very real sense in which a person either has faith or he doesn't. The Bible is constantly dividing humankind into two categories, and only two—the sheep and the goats (Matthew 25:33), the children of God and the children of the devil (1 John 3:10), those who hear and obey and those who merely hear (Matthew 7:24-27), those who shrink back and those who persevere (Hebrews 10:39). You either partake in "faith in Jesus Christ" (Romans 3:22), or you do not.

But there is also a sense in which faith is individual. We are constantly admonished to grow our faith. Faith is one of the attributes listed in 2 Peter 1:5-8 that are to be ours and "increasing." Abraham, the father of the faithful (John 8:39), lived his entire life, as best we can tell, believing that God would direct his paths; however, we read in

Romans 4:19-22 that, after receiving the promises from God, his faith did not stagnate: "Without becoming weak in faith he contemplated his own body, now as good as dead since he was about a hundred years old, and the deadness of Sarah's womb; yet, with respect to the promise of God, he did not waver in unbelief but grew strong in faith, giving glory to God, and being fully assured that what God had promised, He was able also to perform. Therefore it was also credited to him as righteousness." If even Abraham can watch his faith grow, already having left everything he knew to wander in the land of promise (Hebrews 11:8-10), surely we can grow our faith as well.

But how do we do it? The key, it would seem, is looking to see how faith is generated in the first place. Romans 10:17 reads, "So faith comes from hearing, and hearing by the word of Christ." We can only begin a walk of faith by listening to God tell us, through His inspired word, what our first step and all subsequent steps should be. It would seem reasonable, then, that a stronger faith would be found by more of the same—more study, more time in God's word, more wisdom in making application.

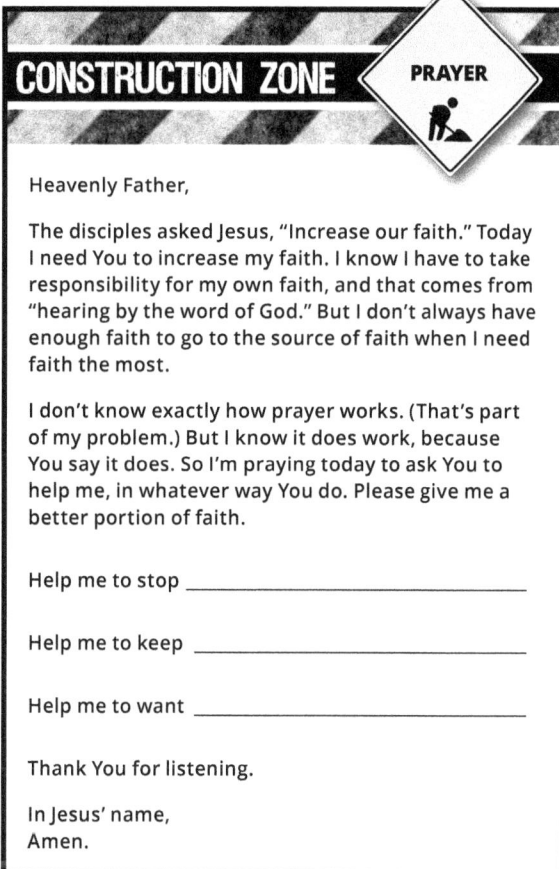

CONSTRUCTION ZONE — PRAYER

Heavenly Father,

The disciples asked Jesus, "Increase our faith." Today I need You to increase my faith. I know I have to take responsibility for my own faith, and that comes from "hearing by the word of God." But I don't always have enough faith to go to the source of faith when I need faith the most.

I don't know exactly how prayer works. (That's part of my problem.) But I know it does work, because You say it does. So I'm praying today to ask You to help me, in whatever way You do. Please give me a better portion of faith.

Help me to stop _____

Help me to keep _____

Help me to want _____

Thank You for listening.

In Jesus' name,
Amen.

Studying God's word will remind us of how powerful God is. He is God Almighty (Genesis 35:11), surely He is worthy of our confidence in days of trial, doubt and discouragement. When Job struggled to find purpose in his sufferings, God supplied him with answers not pertaining to the meaning of suffering but rather to the greatness of the Creator; Job 38:1-7 reads: "Then the Lord answered Job out of the whirlwind and said, 'Who is this that darkens counsel by words without knowledge? Now gird up your loins like a man, and I will ask you, and you instruct Me! Where were you when I laid the foundation of the earth? Tell Me, if you have understanding, who set its measurements? Since you know. Or stretched the line on it? On what were its

Brooke says:

My parents are Christians, so they always figured I would respond to the gospel one day. I guess I always figured I would, too. But they say I need to have a faith of my own. To be honest, I'm not quite sure what that even means.

bases sunk? Or who laid its cornerstone, when the morning stars sang together and all the sons of God shouted for joy?'" The more we investigate the wondrous works of the Creator, the more we are emboldened to accept His will for our lives. He saved the young David and the aged Daniel from lions (1 Samuel 17:34-36, Daniel 6:22); surely He will save us from the greatest lion of all if we resist him (1 Peter 5:8-9).

> **Clyde says:**
>
> After 30 years of being a Christian, I'm not sure I'm that much further along than I was when I started. Even now, I still wonder sometimes whether I believe the Bible, even whether there is a God at all. What's wrong with me?

Studying God's word also will remind us of how loving God is. Surely He is not willing that any should perish (2 Peter 3:9). The gift of His Son on the cross for our salvation should be all the proof we would need in that regard. Page after page in the text tells of His genuine affection for mankind, and particularly His special people. "I have loved you," He tells Israel in Malachi 1:2—a nation that, as Malachi goes on to point out, left a great deal to be desired with respect to their love for Him. His love has nothing to do with our behavior, and we can be grateful for that. It emanates from His character; "The one who does not love does not know God, for God is love" (1 John 4:8). He did not reach out to us because we were loveable; He reached out to us precisely because He knew we would never be loveable. As Paul writes in Romans 5:6-8, "For while we were still helpless, at the right time Christ died for the ungodly. For one will hardly die for a righteous man; though perhaps for the good man someone would dare even to die. But God demonstrates his own love toward us, in that while we were yet sinners, Christ died for us." The more we study, and while doing so look at our own history of rebellion and selfishness, the more overwhelmed we will be at the magnitude of God's emotional commitment to us.

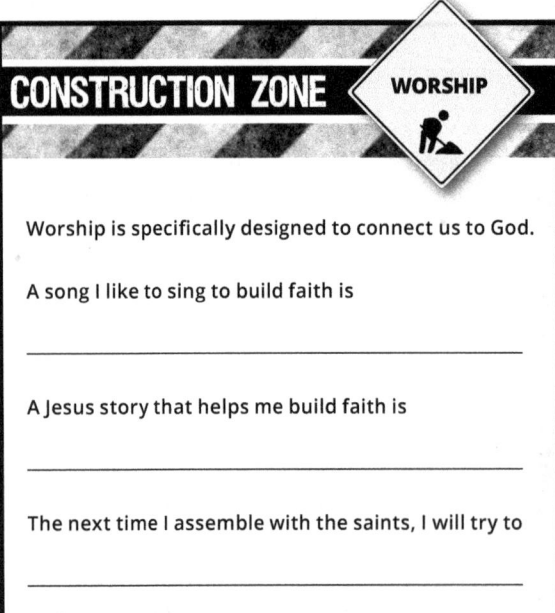

CONSTRUCTION ZONE — WORSHIP

Worship is specifically designed to connect us to God.

A song I like to sing to build faith is

_____

A Jesus story that helps me build faith is

_____

The next time I assemble with the saints, I will try to

_____

But studying God's word also will remind us of how exacting God is. Countless spiritual warriors have fallen by the wayside during their own personal fights, even going so far as to be actively engaged in the battle for the enemy. The prophet Balaam struggled in his personal warfare with materialism, as shown in his dealings with the Moabite king Balak (Numbers 22-24). It is clear he failed; he wound up dying in battle against the Israelites (Joshua 13:22). Surely a donkey would have had more sense than that—and in fact, it did! Regular students of the word will be reminded of those who, to use the Lord's analogy in Luke 9:62, set their hands to the plow only to look back. God has no use for "Christians" of that ilk, and He encourages us constantly to avoid being such.

Some Christians want to wait until they have a full understanding of God's word before they want to share it with others. Perhaps they are afraid they will say something wrong. Perhaps they are afraid the one with whom they are sharing the gospel will have a question they cannot answer.

Don't worry. It will be OK.

In the first place, Christians who have served Jesus for decades will be quick to tell you they do not have as full an understanding as they would like, or that they hope to one day have.

In the second place, you don't need to know everything. You knew enough to come to the Lord yourself; if it was enough for you, it may be enough for someone else.

It is never a mistake to share Jesus with someone who is lost. Remember 1 Corinthians 3:7—"So then neither the one who plants nor the one who waters is anything, but God who causes the growth." Your job is to plant seed, not to save souls. You take care of your job, and let God take care of His.

These and many other attributes of God are things that are well known to any believer. But they are not always in our conscious thoughts, and that can be a burden to us in particularly arduous times of our day, week, year or life. Faith will not only get us through such times, it will grow and blossom within us so that future struggles may be dealt with more easily, with less strain on our minds and souls.

The "finished" product

James tells us that, by enduring trials, we can become "perfect and complete, lacking in nothing" (James 1:4). He means that we will receive everything we need from the hand of God to be successful in every endeavor. But the same apostle Paul who wrote that "the man of God may be adequate, equipped for every good work" (2 Timothy 3:17) also said that he did not consider himself to be finished with his own work, that he was still pressing onward to perfection (Philippians 3:12-14). Is that a contradiction? No, it simply points out that, despite being fully equipped by God, we will always have more work to do. So in that sense, the construction of our faith will never really be "finished."

However, we can, with God's help, proceed in our growth until we find ourselves relying on Him in every aspect of our lives. We can grow out of the day-to-day questions that plague young Christians—why bad things continue to happen to us, why friends are turning on us because of our faith, why "good people" continue to reject the gospel, etc.—and grow into a fuller confidence in God as the ruler of our own lives as well as the lives of all of mankind. "For the kingdom is the Lord's and He rules over the nations" (Psalm 22:28).

14 Building Faith

DISCUSSION

1. How would you respond to Adam? _____
   _____
   _____

2. How would you respond to Brooke? _____
   _____
   _____

3. How would you respond to Clyde? _____
   _____
   _____

LESSON 2

BUILDING TRUST

If you could trade places with one Bible character for one hour, which character and which hour would you choose?

I bet if we polled the church, the winner would wind up being Peter on that stormy night on the Sea of Galilee, as described in Matthew 14:22-33. The sudden shift of emotions from despair to hope to exhilaration. The complete and utter confidence that venturing out onto the surface of the waters—however unprecedented, however impossible—is completely and utterly safe. The Lord is near. How could reaching out to Him possibly be a bad idea.

But trust is a fickle thing. Having enough trust to step out onto the water does not ensure that we will maintain enough trust to finish the trip. Like Peter, we often get distracted by the tempestuous surroundings. We forget about the future because we are consumed with the present. We take our eyes off of Jesus. And we start to sink. Yes, thankfully, Jesus is still there to snatch us up; but we rob ourselves of the joy that we could have had in His presence, replacing blessed memories of triumph with depressing recollections of failure.

Faith and trust are practically synonyms. We distinguish between the two here by saying faith is the assurance of God's existence, Jesus' lordship and heaven's promise; trust here is defined as the confidence that our lives are best lived when lived in praise of the Father, submission to Christ, and the unceasing pursuit of heaven. We have faith in Jesus when we confess Him before men (Romans 10:9-10); we trust in Jesus when we have the confidence to continue to confess Him in our daily lives (Matthew 10:32-33).

The more we live our lives on earth, the more we realize how inadequate we are for every task that really matters. Part of the joy of being a Christian is knowing such issues are taken care of by One who is far more powerful, far more trustworthy. As Paul writes in 2 Corinthians 1:9, "indeed, we had the sentence of death within ourselves so that we would not trust in ourselves, but in God who raises the dead."

We trust Jesus enough to step out of the boat and walk toward Him. No matter how horrible our surroundings, they cannot possibly sink us when Jesus is lifting us up.

Where we start

We all begin cocky, self-assured, brimming with confidence. Most of us, thankfully, survive. We go on to realize the lessons our parents struggled to imprint on our young brains were in fact valuable—that we will make mistakes, that we need help, that our ideas about the world that could not possibly be wrong can be, and usually are, wrong. As Solomon wrote in Proverbs 6:20-22, "My son, observe the commandment of your father and do not forsake the teaching of your mother; bind them continually on your heart; tie them around your neck. When you walk about, they will guide you; when you sleep, they will watch over you; and when you awake, they will talk to you." Judging from what we know of the life of Rehoboam, Solomon's son, Solomon's words of guidance likely fell on deaf ears (as far too many of my father's words did on my ears). Parents trying unsuccessfully to save their children from the mistakes they themselves made in youth—it's an old song, with many, many verses.

Adam says:

So much of the Bible seems counterintuitive to me. Love your enemies? Confess your sins to one another? Turn the other cheek? I'm just not sure I'm ready to put that kind of confidence in God yet. Or in God's people.

If our own wisdom is inadequate to direct our menial, carnal lives, it is far more so with regard to our spiritual lives. One of the verses I quote most often is Jeremiah 10:23—"I know, O Lord, that a man's way is not in himself; nor is it in a man who walks to direct his steps." I quote it often because I need to remind myself often. Decades removed from my impetuous college years, I still remain the arrogant know-it-all far too often. And I don't know it all. Not by a long shot.

But God does.

I came to God for help in my life because I needed it, and because I had confidence He could help. I, perhaps unlike Rehoboam, listen to the wisest man in history when he says in Proverbs 3:5-6, "Trust in the Lord with all your heart and do not lean on your own understanding. In all your ways acknowledge Him, and He will make your paths straight." We "acknowledge Him" by

---

CONSTRUCTION ZONE — PRAYER

Heavenly Father,

I face so many conflicting opinions every day, and so many of them want to take me away from You and the path You have chosen for my life. The wisdom of man is persuasive, and my own thoughts of how things are and how they ought to be often push me in that direction.

I know my life is safe with you. But sometimes I really struggle making decisions in my life that reflect that confidence.

Help me to stop _____

Help me to keep _____

Help me to want _____

Thank You for listening.

In Jesus' name,
Amen.

admitting that He is the voice of reason regarding the way we should conduct ourselves under His sun. When we do it in all our ways—not just the easy ones, not just the obvious ones, not just the convenient ones—we prove ourselves to be His children. "For all who are being led by the Spirit of God, these are sons of God" (Romans 8:14).

How we grow

Getting to the point where we are willing to look to God instead of ourselves for wisdom is a difficult journey. Getting to the point where we do so consistently, in every aspect of our lives, with complete confidence in His guidance—that is a whole other trip, one fraught with pot holes, detours and misleading information.

We all have friends who call themselves Christians but do not govern certain parts of their lives by God's will. Perhaps it's their marriages. Perhaps it's their entertainment. Perhaps it's their language. Whatever the particulars, we have all approached those friends and suggested they read what the Bible has to say on the subject. And generally our friends chuckle and say, "You're right, I should do that" (implying clearly that they have no intention of doing so), or, "I tried that, and the problem just got worse," or, "That may have worked back in Paul's day, but this is 21st Century America; things are different now."

But if we were honest with ourselves during our criticisms of others, we would admit the same advice works just as well for us in our struggles. The Bible addresses issues of our daily lives such as gossip, lying, attire, finances and child-rearing—subjects that we have all studied a dozen times, perhaps a hundred times. And the Bible reads the same way every time. But instead of heeding the advice of the Lord, we conjure up excuses for implementing the solutions we found by consulting worldly sources of wisdom such as peers, self-help books, and trial and error. And our dismissal of Bible-based advice sounds remarkably similar to the responses of our friends in the world to our suggestions. Is the pot calling the kettle black? Perhaps so.

Brooke says:

My best friend stabbed me in the back once. I never saw it coming. It took me months before I could even look him in the eye. And he calls himself a Christian! How can I be sure my "brethren" in the church really have my back?

If we trusted in the Lord enough to give him our hearts in the beginning, is it not reasonable to continue to trust Him while we are living lives in His service? God's word is truth (John 17:17); it would have to be, since God Himself cannot lie (Titus 1:2). So if that word required us to wash away our sins in the act of baptism (Acts 22:16) and we believed and obeyed, surely we should have confidence enough to "overcome evil with good" (Romans 12:21), or turn the other cheek (Matthew 5:39), or forgive repeatedly (Matthew 18:21-22).

We are constantly offered "fixes" for the problems of life—sometimes offered by brethren, sometimes propped up with Scripture—that at their root eat away at the trust we are to place in God and His word. But simply being "brethren" did not lend

> **CONSTRUCTION ZONE — WORSHIP**
>
> Worship is specifically designed to connect us to God.
>
> A song I like to sing to build trust is
>
> _____
>
> A Jesus story that helps me build trust is
>
> _____
>
> The next time I assemble with the saints, I will try to
>
> _____

credence to Hymenaeus and Philetus, false teachers known to Paul (2 Timothy 2:16-18); their work eroded the faith of Christians rather than enhancing it. And simply quoting Scripture in defense of one's heresy is no panacea; even the devil can do that (Matthew 4:6). But ultimately, we will be given an opportunity to either trust God or trust the false teacher. And when the latter begins arguments with phrases such as, "I know the Bible says that, but I really think ...," he is self-condemned. Heed the words of Paul in such cases: "Now I urge you, brethren, keep your eye on those who cause dissensions and hindrances contrary to the teaching which you learned, and turn away from them. For such men are slaves, not of our Lord Christ but of their own appetites; and by their smooth and flattering speech they deceive the hearts of the unsuspecting" (Romans 16:17-18).

The "finished" product

One of the truly astonishing things about the God we serve is His absolute trustworthiness. We say sometimes, "No one knows what the future holds." But that's not true. God knows. And because of that, and a thousand other things, I can trust that my future is safe with Him. No matter what may come, obedience to His word and hope in His future will get me through.

Remember 1 John 3:19-22—"We will know by this that we are of the truth, and will assure our heart before Him in whatever our heart condemns us; for God is greater than our heart and knows all things. Beloved, if our heart does not condemn us, we have confidence before God; and whatever we ask we receive from Him, because we keep His commandments and do the things that are pleasing in His sight."

> **Clyde says:**
>
> *I used to have confidence in brethren. But I've learned through bitter experience that elders will fail you, preachers will fail you, even spouses will fail you. It's happened to me more times than I can count. Surely this isn't just me.*

Being a Christian means no longer being a slave to our own weaknesses and failures. It means knowing our lives are on the right course, knowing God forgives us, knowing He is supplying us with everything we will need. Surely we can say with the psalmist in Psalm 56:11, "In God I have put my trust, I shall not be afraid. What can man do to me?"

Mankind, of course, does not know the future. And so the trustworthiness of humans is necessarily unreliable. I love the sarcastic tone of the prophet's words to the arrogant in Isaiah 41:23-24—"Declare the things that are going to come afterward, that we may know that you are gods; indeed, do good or evil, that we may anxiously look about us and fear together. Behold, you are of no account, and your work amounts to nothing; he who chooses you is an abomination." What sort of person who claims to believe in God would choose to trust a human being?

I would, and you can too—that is, if the human being in question is a Christian. No, he or she won't be perfect. But I can have confidence that the same power pushing me toward the example of Jesus Christ is working in them as well. Love "believes all things," according to 1 Corinthians 13:7. That same bond of fellowship that ties me to my Savior ties me also to my brethren. I can assume they are worthy of my trust because we are part of the same body (1 Corinthians 12:12-13) and we are working together for a common goal.

Yes, brethren will let me down from time to time. But usually those will be accidental missteps—easily forgiven, quickly forgotten. True, we occasionally will be stabbed in the back by a brother in Christ; as the psalmist complains in Psalm 55:12-14, "For it is not an enemy who reproaches me, then I could bear it; nor is it one who hates me who has exalted himself against me, then I could hide myself from him. But it is you, a man my equal, my companion and my familiar friend; we who had sweet fellowship together walked in the house of God in the throng." But even in these situations, God is with us, holding us up, supremely and consistently trustworthy. And as long as He has my confidence, I can withstand the betrayals of even the closest of friends and family.

CONSTRUCTION ZONE — EVANGELISM

Jesus told His closest disciples in Matthew 10:19-20, "But when they hand you over, do not worry about how or what you are to say; for it will be given you in that hour what you are to say. For it is not you who speak, but it is the Spirit of your Father who speaks in you."

He did not, however, tell us that. And sometimes, when we are trying to find the right thing to say in defense of His gospel, we wish we were partakers of the Spirit in the same way as the apostles were.

But we are, essentially. Although it was the apostles who were guided into the truth directly by the Spirit (John 16:13), we are guided every bit as much today as they were then. "The foundation of the apostles and prophets" (Ephesians 2:20) was the only gospel acceptable in the New Testament era, and the preaching of another gospel was condemned (Galatians 1:8-9). That First Century gospel is the gospel we have preserved for us today in the New Testament, the one that was "once for all handed down to the saints" (Jude 3).

The gospel is God's down payment on our salvation, a token of His commitment to save us (Ephesians 1:13-14). If we can trust Him, we can trust His word.

DISCUSSION

1. How would you respond to Adam? _____
   _____
   _____

2. How would you respond to Brooke? _____
   _____
   _____

3. How would you respond to Clyde? _____
   _____
   _____

LESSON 3

BUILDING HOPE

Some people cross their fingers. Some people wish on a star. Some people throw coins into fountains. But they all have something in common: they have an unfortunate situation in their lives that they would like to exchange for a better one.

But few could claim to be suffering a day worse than the day this man was having. He was in the process of dying for his crimes—and since his crimes moved Pilate to put him on a cross, it's reasonable to assume his crimes were substantial. But the longer he hung on the cross, the more attention he gave to one of his companions in misery—someone, surely, who was suffering as much as he, yet doing so with the utmost grace and dignity.

Finally, the railing (which, according to Matthew 27:44, he appears to have been a part of in the beginning) became too much. And he said to his fellow criminal, "Do you not even fear God, since you are under the same sentence of condemnation? And we indeed are suffering justly, for we are receiving what we deserve for our deeds; but this man has done nothing wrong" (Luke 23:40-41). And, despite the appearance of complete, utter failure on the part of the one mockingly proclaimed as "The King of the Jews," he still found enough faith to say to Him, "Jesus, remember me when You come in Your kingdom!" And Jesus responded, "Truly I say to you, today you shall be with Me in Paradise" (Luke 23:42-43).

Adam says:

The preacher makes heaven sound wonderful and hell sound horrible. But it seems like we have plenty of heaven and hell here already. Shouldn't we be spending less effort on the next life and more on this one?

Hope does not, as the poet Alexander Pope wrote, spring eternal—not for everyone, anyway. People trade hope for despair daily. The horrors of disease, injustice, terror, pain and suffering create debilitating depression in some, and even move others to end their own lives prematurely. Yet hope is a concept instilled in us by God. We tear up when we hear Little Orphan Annie singing, "The sun will come out tomorrow." We want to believe. We need to believe.

And God gives us something to believe in.

Where we start

We practically come into this life thinking about the next one. Solomon wrote in Ecclesiastes 3:11, "He has made everything appropriate in its time. He has also set eternity in their heart, yet so that man will not find out the work which God has done from the beginning even to the end." We know intuitively that it makes no sense that existence should end with death. And left to ourselves, we have concocted a wide variety of theories to fill the heaven-shaped void in our hearts. Philosophers, poets and prophets have proposed one thing after another. The Hindus believe in reincarnation. The Vikings envisioned their warriors joyfully hacking one another to bits all day long, only to wake up in the morning completely healed, ready to go again. But historically, hardly any culture at all believed that after death we were just like Rover, dead all over.

> **CONSTRUCTION ZONE — PRAYER**
>
> Heavenly Father,
>
> This life is full of trouble and hardship. I thank You and praise You for the life that is waiting for me after this one is over. You cannot lie, and you have promised to save Your faithful ones in heaven. So as wonderful as many of the things here on earth are, my true hope is to leave it one day to be with You and the saved ones of all the ages.
>
> Help me to stop _____
>
> Help me to keep _____
>
> Help me to want _____
>
> Thank You for listening.
>
> In Jesus' name,
> Amen.

God did not intend for us to search our personal stores of wisdom to find what eternity might be like. He planned for us to listen to Him tell us about eternity, to believe that there could be nothing more beautiful than an unending day spent in complete fellowship with Him. This is His plan. This is what He has revealed to us. This is where we find our hope.

Paul tells us in Colossians 3:1-4, "Therefore if you have been raised up with Christ, keep seeking the things above, where Christ is, seated at the right hand of God. Set your mind on the things above, not on the things that are on earth. For you have died and your life is hidden with Christ in God. When Christ, who is our life, is revealed, then you also will be revealed with Him in glory." We didn't come to Jesus because we wanted to have more hope in this life; we came because we realized hope in this life is meaningless, and that we wanted something more. And "more" is exactly what Jesus offers. Bitter experience has convinced us that this life, even in the best of circumstances, cannot possibly hold enough for us. We, like the thief of

> **Brooke says:**
>
> *They say heaven is wonderful. We sure sing about it often enough. But if I am honest, I have to admit I'm looking forward more to our family vacation this summer. I know that isn't right. What am I supposed to do?*

old, want Paradise. And we have come to believe that Jesus is the way to get there—the only way (John 14:6).

How we grow

We thrill at the notion of complete and permanent fellowship with God, Jesus, the Spirit, and the faithful of all ages. But this hope does not immobilize us in this life; far from it. After emphasizing the glories waiting for us after this life is over, the apostle goes on to say in 1 John 3:3, "And everyone who has this hope fixed on Him purifies himself, just as He is pure." By fixing our eyes on, "the author and perfecter of faith" (Hebrews 12:2), we learn more and more what true purity is. And as we learn to exemplify that purity in this life, and chafe at our repeated failures in our pursuit of our mark, we find our hope growing. We do not grow discouraged at our shortcomings. We rejoice in the Lord that He offers us grace and mercy, and we long even more for the time when such corrective measures will not be necessary.

Setting our minds on Christ is a daily, even hourly, decision we make. We wake up in the morning and decide to pursue holiness. We lie down at night and reflect on our failures and successes. In between, we evaluate every circumstance in our lives, new and old, with a view toward our relationship with Jesus. We admire business leaders who pursue financial success with a single-minded purpose. Athletes in pursuit of a championship receive the same commendation. We may not share their goals, but we appreciate the attitude that drives them toward success as they define it. The hope set before them motivates them to behave in such a way as to maximize the possibility of achieving the hope. We do the same thing as Christians—except our hope is far grander than theirs.

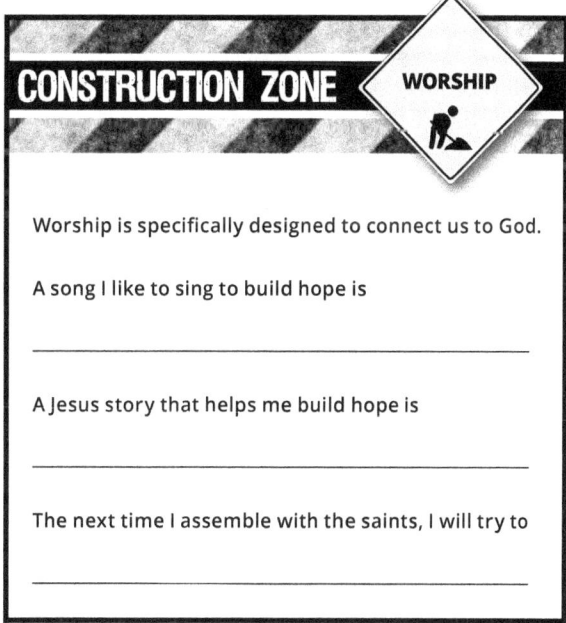

Growing our hope is best done by developing daily habits that take our attention away from the issues of this life that may seem pressing at the time. Issues regarding finances, politics, education, and personal achievement of all sorts can become overwhelming; indeed, the accolades heaped upon business leaders, athletes and other high achievers may persuade us that hoping in this life is the key to success. But if we think that way, it is for the same reason the world thinks that way—we have our hope centered in the wrong place. So when we find ourselves drifting in that direction, we reorient ourselves. We come to realize the truth of Paul's words in 1 Corinthians 15:19—"If we have hoped in Christ in this life only, we are of all men most to be pitied." The "hope of His calling" (Ephesians 1:18), the "hope of glory" (Colossians 1:27), the "hope of salvation" (1 Thessalonians 5:8)—this is far too grand to be contained within three dimensions, or even within time. Only eternity is large enough to contain the "hope of eternal life" (Titus 3:7).

So eternity is where we look, even when times are difficult. Especially then. We take as our examples the sojourners in the land of Canaan. They wandered, living in tents, never having a permanent dwelling—not just because God had promised something more stable to future generations, but also because He had promised something more stable to them. "All these died in faith, without receiving the promises, but having seen them and having welcomed them from a distance, and having confessed that they were strangers and exiles on the earth. For those who say such things make it clear that they are seeking a country of their own. And indeed if they had been thinking of that country from which they went out, they would have had opportunity to return. But as it is, they desire a better country, that is, a heavenly one. Therefore God is not ashamed to be called their God; for He has prepared a city for them" (Hebrews 11:13-16).

We, too, are exiles. "Our citizenship is in heaven" (Philippians 3:20), not here on earth. We are stranded in a strange land, surrounded by strange people with strange customs and a strange language. And we fiercely cling to our hope that God will bring us home one day.

The "finished" product

Jeremiah was surrounded by the wreckage that his people had made of themselves. He himself was God's vessel to tell them they would have to spend 70 years in Babylonian exile to atone for their sins. But Jeremiah, like many other prophets of doom, also is given words of encouragement to share with those who would choose to grow from the experience. We read in Jeremiah 29:10-11, "For thus says the Lord, 'When seventy years have been completed for Babylon, I will visit you and fulfill My good word to you, to bring you back to this place. For I know the plans that I have for you,' declares

CONSTRUCTION ZONE — EVANGELISM

In his defense before Felix (Acts 24:14-21), Paul characterized himself as having "a hope in God ... that there shall certainly be a resurrection of both the righteous and the wicked." This hope, he said, motivated him to "maintain always a blameless conscience both before God and before men." He knew a day of reckoning was coming for all of mankind. And he was fully confident that, if he would continue the walk with Christ he had begun, it would end in glory.

Despite Paul's best efforts, Felix could not bring himself to share this hope. In their later discussion, Paul spoke frankly about "righteousness, self-control and the judgment to come" (Acts 24:25), but it was not enough to persuade Felix to leave his self-centered, lascivious lifestyle. He made his excuses to Paul and ended the conversation.

Such will be the case with many souls with whom we share the gospel. We can prick the souls of men with the gospel (Acts 2:37), but we cannot compel them to obey. All we can do is share our hope with them, and do it with enough conviction that they will be motivated to examine it themselves.

the Lord, 'plans for welfare and not for calamity to give you a future and a hope.'" Even at their lowest ebb, the Israelites were able to look to the future and see the glory God had planned for them. But they would have to look.

We as Christians choose to look. We accept by faith the future God has for us—a future, like theirs, which is "for welfare and not for calamity." We also have roughly 70 years of exile (Psalm 90:10). And the longer we stay here, the closer we get to home. We could choose to let our hope die—to forget about God's future and say with the unbelievers, "Let us eat and drink, for tomorrow we die" (1 Corinthians 15:32). But Jesus through His resurrection has given us "a living hope" (1 Peter 1:3). This hope springs alive anew every day, motivated in His cause, alert to the trials and temptations that would distract us. "Do this, knowing the time, that it is already the hour for you to awaken from sleep; for now salvation is nearer to us than when we first believed" (Romans 13:11).

Clyde says:

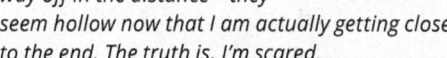

I find myself thinking about death a lot more often these days. All those things I said about heaven when it was way off in the distance—they seem hollow now that I am actually getting close to the end. The truth is, I'm scared.

Our hope lives because our Savior lives. And because He lives, we can say with David in Psalm 39:7, "My hope is in You." Hiding our lives with God in Christ is the gesture He requires us to make to show how strong our hope is of heaven, how much we yearn for it, how fervently we pray with John in Revelation 22:20, "Amen. Come, Lord Jesus."

This is our hope. And truly, as Paul reminds us in Romans 5:5, "hope does not disappoint."

DISCUSSION

1. How would you respond to Adam? _____
   _____
   _____

2. How would you respond to Brooke? _____
   _____
   _____

3. How would you respond to Clyde? _____
   _____
   _____

LESSON 4

BUILDING LOVE

What if you lost a prized possession? What if it were something that was so important to you that you would forget about everything you still had and put your entire life on hold just so you could relocate it? And what if, at the end of the day, it turned up? You would be so excited, you would immediately text-message all your friends, Tweet, post on Facebook, do whatever you do to get in touch with as many friends as possible as quickly as possible. The thing you loved so much was back!

What if, instead of just one possession, it was your retirement account? Ten percent of everything you had earned for your entire working life was gone in an instant. You would call your accountant immediately. You would get out all your tax returns and cancelled checks. You would go through your bank statements with a fine-toothed comb. And if in the end you realized it was just a computer error or, more likely, an arithmetic error on your end, you would be immensely relieved. Text, Tweet, post, the whole drill.

Now, what if it were not a single possession that was lost? What if it were not just money?

What if it were your child?

Jesus tells us, in His beautiful trio of parables found in Luke 15, that the Father's love for His children is like that. It grieves Him when we are lost. It gives Him immeasurable joy when we are found.

Jesus also tells us, particularly in the third of the parables, that we often do not have that same sort of love for one another. And we have no excuse. The perfect example of love has been provided for us—"But God demonstrates his own love toward us, in that while we were yet sinners, Christ died for us" (Romans 5:8). Repeatedly we are told to love our brethren (Hebrews 13:1), to love our neighbors (James 2:8), even to love our enemies (Matthew 5:44). God's will on the matter is clear. The question is, how important is it to us that we obey it?

Where we start

People define love in different ways. So does the Bible. Occasionally the text refers to romantic love, as with Isaac's love for Rebekah (Genesis 24:67). Also there is the familial love or "natural affection" (or, more accurately, the lack thereof) to which Paul refers in Romans 1:31 and 2 Timothy 3:3. But generally love falls into two categories—emotional and unemotional. The emotional, *phileo* love is that which binds close friends together (Romans 12:10, Hebrews 13:1). It is not typically used to characterize our relationship with God. In fact, *phileo* and its derivatives are only used in reference to God a handful of times. Jesus calls His disciples friends in John 15:14-15; Abraham is called "the friend of God" in James 2:23; Peter is asked in the third exchange with the Lord whether he has *phileo* for Him, and Peter confirms that he does (John 21:17); and Paul warns those who would not be warm-hearted toward the Lord in 1 Corinthians 16:22—"If anyone does not love the Lord, he is to be accursed. Maranatha." More typically, it appears in the text as "love of the brethren" or "brotherly kindness," as in 1 Peter 1:22 and 2 Peter 1:7.

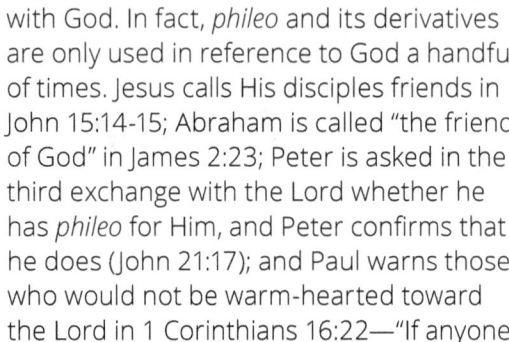

Adam says:

I barely know these people. And now I'm supposed to love them? I haven't even had a chance to decide whether I even like them. And if "love your neighbor" means what my old friends seem to think, forget it. I'll pass.

The far more common "love" in the New Testament is *agapeo*. It refers to a selfless approach toward someone, one that pursues another's interest and welfare. This is the love the Lord says we must have first for God, and then for our neighbors (Matthew 22:37-39). It is the love God has for us and that He requires us to emulate in our relations with others (Matthew 5:46-48), particularly our brethren (1 John 4:11).

God doesn't have to command us to have friendly relations; it is instinctive. And He does not require us to have the same affection toward friends, family, strangers and enemies alike; that is impossible. He does, however, command us to have regard for all humanity—to value every human life, to seek good for all, to desire their salvation as fervently as He does (1 Timothy 2:4).

The problem with that kind of love is, we are too busy already loving ourselves. Our own welfare is of

CONSTRUCTION ZONE — PRAYER

Heavenly Father,

You tell us over and over again to love one another. But it is difficult for me, especially with people who don't love me and don't especially care if I know it. Even among Your people, love sometimes seems difficult to come by. And I know I give people far too much excuse to not show me the love I expect from them.

You showed more love than I can imagine when You sent Jesus to the cross for us. And You continue to show that love every day of my life. I need to find a way to show that love in my life, and I need to feel it from others.

Help me to stop _____

Help me to keep _____

Help me to want _____

Thank You for listening.

In Jesus' name,
Amen.

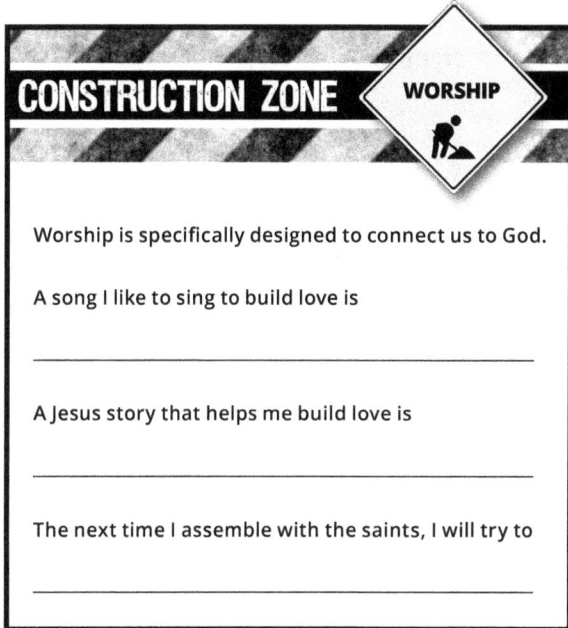

CONSTRUCTION ZONE — WORSHIP

Worship is specifically designed to connect us to God.

A song I like to sing to build love is

_____

A Jesus story that helps me build love is

_____

The next time I assemble with the saints, I will try to

_____

paramount importance. That also is instinctive. But that instinct is something that we can and must overcome. Pursuing personal interests first would never have allowed Jesus to go to the cross, or allowed His Father to send Him there. They chose to put sinful mankind first. And we are required to do no less. "Do nothing from selfishness or empty conceit, but with humility of mind regard one another as more important than yourselves; do not merely look out for your own personal interests, but also for the interests of others. Have this attitude in yourselves which was also in Christ Jesus, who, although He existed in the form of God, did not regard equality with God a thing to be grasped, but emptied himself, taking the form of a bond-servant, and being made in the likeness of men" (Philippians 2:3-7).

How we grow

The longer we live on earth, the more aware we are of how unworthy of love our neighbors typically are. Certainly some may distinguish themselves from time to time. When someone does something remarkable, particularly in our service, it naturally raises them in our estimation. But we will also find that every one of them, regardless of how noble they may be, will act in a hateful, neglectful or dismissive fashion. And most of the time that we notice such things, we are the victims of their behavior. Truly we are all "under sin" (Romans 3:9).

Brooke says:

I don't like talking about love. Mention the L word and everyone goes crazy with gossip and drama. I didn't come to Jesus to find a soul mate. I don't need that. You know what I actually need? A really good friend or two.

But God knew that long before we did. And He loved them anyway, each and every one. He loved not because of who they were, but because of who He is. It is His nature; "God is love" (1 John 4:8). It is not, however, our nature. We have to change. "As obedient children, do not be conformed to the former lusts which were yours in your ignorance, but like the Holy One who called you, be holy yourselves also in all your behavior; because it is written, 'You shall be holy, for I am holy'" (1 Peter 1:14-16).

So, as with all our behavior, learning to love begins with the desire to be like God. And with that foundation, we learn not to allow our neighbors' merits and demerits factor into the discussion. We do not love them because of who they are; we love them because of who we are. Naturally we do not rejoice when people demonstrate themselves to be unlovely; naturally such an attitude will affect whether we can cultivate an emotion-based friendship with them. But it has nothing to do with the love God requires us to have for them.

Clyde says:

I'm just not an emotional kind of person. I don't like talking about my feelings. And when others get emotional with me, I become very uncomfortable. Does that make me unloving? Because I'm not sure how much I can change.

We can reasonably expect a better, more encouraging result when we extend love to brothers and sisters in Christ. Derivatives of *phileo* are found twice in Romans 12:10—"Be devoted to one another in brotherly love." One would think that the common bond we share in the Lord would extend beyond simply extending unemotional good will to one another, that we would develop genuine affection for one another. Such is not always the case, unfortunately. Brethren, too, will show themselves to be less than perfect. But as a rule, Christians choosing individually to pursue the things of Jesus in their own lives will develop brotherly connections in the process. The apostle indicates as much in 1 John 1:7—"but if we walk in the Light as He Himself is in the Light, we have fellowship with one another, and the blood of Jesus His Son cleanses us from all sin." Fellowship is a natural result of our mutual pursuit of Jesus, John says. And if the Lord can forgive our missteps along the way, surely we can find it in ourselves to forgive one another.

CONSTRUCTION ZONE — EVANGELISM

People who love fish make the best fishermen. Most people are turned off at the prospect of actually coming in contact with a slimy, squirmy, perhaps prickly creature. And the fish aren't any less so on the line or in the boat of the ace fisherman. But he accepts that as the nature of fish, and he doesn't love them any less for it.

Besides loving fish, the most important thing is loving the act of fishing. Anyone can love pulling in a big catch and putting it on the deck. Anyone can love having his picture taken with it. But the great ones are thrilled with the prospect, not just with the success. They don't go fishing because they *will* catch fish; it is enough for them to know that they *might*.

As "fishers of men" (Matthew 4:19), we are not required to save everyone—or save anyone, for that matter. That's God's job. Our job is to put the net in the water and (pardon the mixed metaphor) let God give the increase. Loving our neighbors as ourselves (Matthew 22:39); if it means anything, means acting to save their souls. If we are unwilling to do that, if we even consciously pass on opportunities to do so, we don't love fish enough.

The "finished" product

How much love is enough? At what point do you think you have maxed out in your attachment to your friends, your children, your spouse? At what point in your relationship with anyone truly important in your life did you say, "That's close enough"? Doesn't the importance of the relationship necessarily infer that you will want to continue to draw near to them?

Certainly that should be the case with regard to our love for God. Loving with all of our heart, soul, mind and strength does not mean there is a point of absolute saturation, when we actually achieve "all" and have nothing else to give. Or if there is such a point, it is reasonable to assume we, as imperfect lovers, have not gotten there yet and never will. We must continue to pray, borrowing from Psalm 86:11, "Unite my heart to fear Your name." Every nook and cranny of our heart should be given over to the pursuit of God and His purposes for our lives.

As we learn to love God more perfectly, we learn to love one another as well. The perceived slights we suffer at one another's hands mean less and less. Surely the inconvenience (and it is seldom more than that) caused by a brother in Christ, consciously or unconsciously, is not worth the emphasis we give it in pursuit of whatever form of justice to which we may feel entitled. "Why not rather be wronged?" Paul asks in 1 Corinthians 6:7. "Why not rather be defrauded?"

Try this exercise: read the familiar text on love in 1 Corinthians 13, going from verse 4 through the beginning of verse 8—but insert your own name where you see the word "love." See how you measure up. Hal is patient. Hal is kind and is not jealous. Hal does not brag and is not arrogant. Hal bears all things, believes all things, hopes all things, endures all things. Hal never fails. Does our love look like that? And if not, why not?

DISCUSSION

1. How would you respond to Adam? _____
   _____
   _____

2. How would you respond to Brooke? _____
   _____
   _____

3. How would you respond to Clyde? _____
   _____
   _____

LESSON 5

BUILDING DESIRE

The young man had it all. Popularity. Cultural significance. Youth. Health. And, of course, money. Lots of money. But none of it mattered to him in comparison to his relationship with God.

That is, until he actually had to choose between the two.

The entire episode baffled the disciples. The so-called "rich young ruler" had everything they did not—everything they were brought up to believe was important in life. And it's not like he had abandoned spiritual pursuits entirely in his quest for what the world had to offer him in this life; far from it. According to his own testimony, anyway—and we have no reason to doubt him—he had kept God's commandments from his youth (Mark 10:20). He was the man every mother in the synagogue pointed to and told her young sons to aspire to be.

And apparently, that wasn't good enough for Jesus.

He just didn't want to follow the Lord as much as Peter and the rest of the Lord's close disciples did. Granted, Peter did not have nearly as much to leave as the rich young ruler did; but whatever it was, however much of it there was, he left it—and so did the rest of the disciples (Mark 10:28). It was what they wanted to do. It was the only thing they wanted to do.

Adam says:

Do I want to go to hell? Of course not! And I'll do what it takes to not go there. But how can I just flip a switch and suddenly want to serve Jesus as much as I've always wanted physical things? And I still want them, by the way.

That is the kind of person Jesus wants. The ability doesn't matter. The reputation doesn't matter. The money certainly doesn't matter. All He wants is our heart. If we can manage to give Him that, the rest will take care of itself. And the wonderful thing about it is, every one of us is capable of giving Him that. I could not give Him a million dollars any more than I could give Him a symphony or a cure for cancer. But I can give him my heart. And so can you.

He has left no doubt regarding how much He desires a relationship with us. The real question is, how much do we desire a relationship with Him?

Where we start

We live in a three-dimensional world, surrounded by things we see, touch, taste, smell and hear. These are the things we naturally crave. And that is not necessarily a problem. But it becomes a problem when our pursuit of physical things interferes with our pursuit of the things of God. And that's the way we were before we knew Jesus: "Among them we too all formerly lived in the lusts of our flesh, indulging the desires of the flesh and of the mind, and were by nature children of wrath, even as the rest" (Ephesians 2:3). We didn't know any better. That carnal nature of ours was interfering with our pursuit of heavenly things—not because we were incapable of spirituality, mind you, but because we were still choosing to spurn the Spirit of God for the spirit of the world, and because of that we were not willing to open our ears to Him (1 Corinthians 2:12-14).

Thankfully, we came to our senses. We realized there was more for us than just what we perceive. And "more" was exactly what we wanted. Dissatisfied with the things the world has to offer us—as enticing as those things are—we chose to embrace an invisible world of the spirit in pursuit of the invisible blessings God promises to provide for us there.

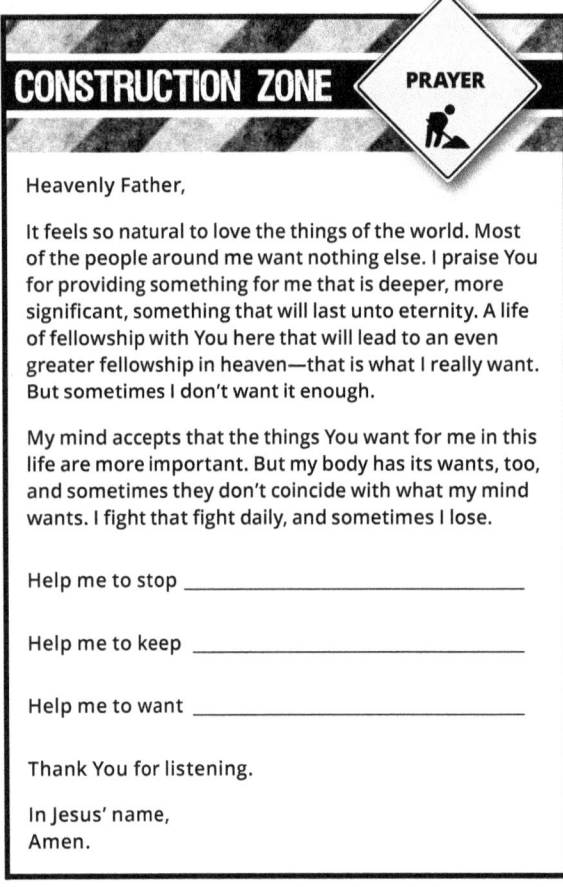

CONSTRUCTION ZONE — **PRAYER**

Heavenly Father,

It feels so natural to love the things of the world. Most of the people around me want nothing else. I praise You for providing something for me that is deeper, more significant, something that will last unto eternity. A life of fellowship with You here that will lead to an even greater fellowship in heaven—that is what I really want. But sometimes I don't want it enough.

My mind accepts that the things You want for me in this life are more important. But my body has its wants, too, and sometimes they don't coincide with what my mind wants. I fight that fight daily, and sometimes I lose.

Help me to stop _____

Help me to keep _____

Help me to want _____

Thank You for listening.

In Jesus' name,
Amen.

But learning to truly love spiritual things more than physical things is an acquired ability. We receive 24-hour-a-day training in regard to loving the things in the physical world. And if we allow our affections to drift away from the things of God, we run the risk of drifting away ourselves. It happened to Demas, who "loved this present world" (2 Timothy 4:10). And many Christians have followed in his footsteps—including many preachers.

To make matters worse, some of the desires we encounter in this life are designed by the devil, intended specifically to take our eyes off our heavenly prize. As 1 John 2:15-

17 reminds us, "Do not love the world nor the things in the world. If anyone loves the world, the love of the Father is not in him. For all that is in the world, the lust of the flesh and the lust of the eyes and the boastful pride of life, is not from the Father, but is from the world. The world is passing away, and also its lusts; but the one who does the will of God lives forever." God gives us examples of rebellion in the Bible, "so that we would not crave evil things as they also craved" (1 Corinthians 10:6). The quicker we learn discipline in such matters, the easier it will become to say no to sin in the future.

Brooke says:

I want pizza for dinner. I want that outfit, that download, and that grade. That's the sort of thing I automatically think of when people ask me what I want. Shouldn't I be thinking more about spiritual things?

How we grow

We all set priorities in our lives. Work before play. Family before strangers. Sleep before the late movie. Certain needs must be met before certain other needs. God has no problem with us catering to the physical issues of life. But He does not want them to become our primary desire. If I want to play more than work, I run the risk of losing my job—and with it, the money I use to play. And if I want physical gratification before spiritual exaltation, I run the risk of losing everything I have in store in heaven. That's especially insane, considering I am going to lose all the physical things eventually as well: "For we have brought nothing into the world, so we cannot take anything out of it either" (1 Timothy 6:7).

The key, then, is to feed our soul first and our body second.

Tragically, not all Christians think this way. Paul writes in Philippians 3:18-19, "For many walk, of whom I often told you, and now tell you even weeping, that they are enemies of the cross of Christ, whose end is destruction, whose god is their appetite, and whose glory is their shame, who set their mind on earthly things." And he is not talking about outsiders in this context; these are brothers and sisters in Christ who have forgotten their heavenly calling in their pursuit of earthly gratification. They are the Lord's enemies, he says. And they are our enemies as well if we allow them to taint our perception of service to Christ, making us believe we can put our own comforts and conveniences ahead of our spiritual responsibility.

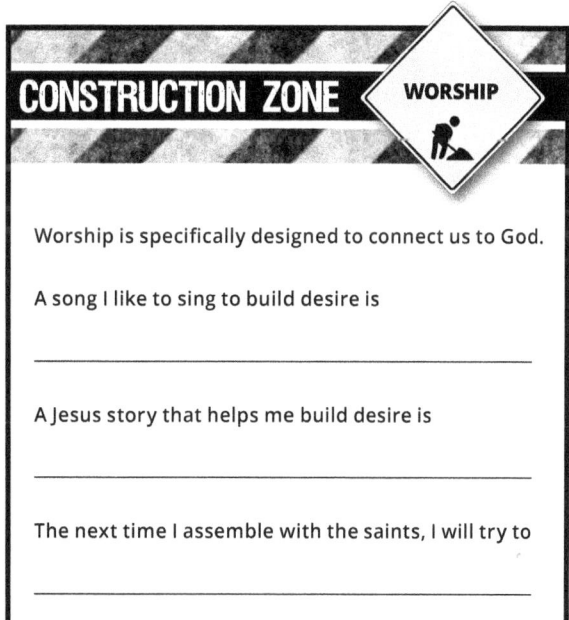

CONSTRUCTION ZONE — WORSHIP

Worship is specifically designed to connect us to God.

A song I like to sing to build desire is

_____

A Jesus story that helps me build desire is

_____

The next time I assemble with the saints, I will try to

_____

Choices of fleshly over heavenly demonstrate our true loyalties. God wants us to see this world as a way station, a place to pitch our tents temporarily while we await transport to our permanent dwelling. And since we are so completely out of place here, it is not surprising that we should feel uncomfortable. Paul in 2 Corinthians 5:1-4 reminds us that the discomforts and inconveniences of this life are intended to make us less devoted to the things of this life, more focused on the life to come: "For we know that if the earthly tent which is our house is torn down, we have a building from God, a house not made with hands, eternal in the heavens. For indeed in this house we groan, longing to be clothed with our dwelling from heaven, inasmuch as we, having put it on, will not be found naked. For indeed, while we are in this tent, we groan, being burdened, because we do not want to be unclothed but to be clothed, so that what is mortal will be swallowed up by life." Truly, as we often sing, "This world is not my home, I'm just a-passing through."

> **Clyde says:**
> I'm tired. I've put in plenty of time in the Lord's service. And I'm not saying I'm going to quit now. I'm not. But to tell the truth, it's hard to work up enthusiasm for the Christian life like I did when I was younger.

But instead of yearning for our permanent home, often we find we have fallen in love with our prison cell. We obsess over how we can make our bed softer, or our pillow fluffier, or our walls brighter, or our view better, or our neighbor quieter, or our jailer kinder—as though this is some sort of permanent arrangement, as though we belong here. What we really ought to be doing is spending every waking and sleeping moment here dreaming about the day we are going to get out.

I'm going home one day. I can't afford to forget about that. Not for one moment. That is my greatest and ultimate desire.

CONSTRUCTION ZONE — EVANGELISM

Why is it that we do not talk more to our friends about Jesus? Perhaps it is because we value the relationship we already have with them, and we are hesitant to risk it. Yes, adding a spiritual fellowship on top of the existing bond would be a wonderful thing. But if the relationship is already wonderful, perhaps we are content with half a loaf.

What is our desire with regard to our loved ones? Surely we would say, first and foremost, their salvation. But if that is true, surely every interaction we have with them would be in pursuit of that objective. Certainly we would not want to do anything to make them content or comfortable in a lost state. But is that, in fact, exactly what we are doing?

No single approach is appropriate for every Christian and every relationship. And certainly the time comes occasionally for us to shake the dust off our feet (Matthew 10:14). But we should not come to that extreme conclusion lightly—certainly not just because we are afraid of hurting their feelings. If we avoid telling them about Jesus simply out of fear, perhaps we desire their friendship more than their salvation.

The "finished" product

It is a "better country" we desire (Hebrews 11:16)—not just a better version of this country. And the longer we live in pursuit of God's promised land, the more we realize the life here is incompatible with it. We find the things here on earth that give us the most joy are the ones that give us a foretaste of the joys yet to come. Yes, we desire them—because they bring us that much closer to our true desire.

We also put into perspective the purely physical things of this life. We can delight in the birth of a child because it reminds us that life itself is a gift from God and is intended to be lived in His service (Ecclesiastes 12:13). We can delight in our "daily bread" because it reminds us of God's constant care over us (Deuteronomy 8:3) and of His greater, spiritual provision (John 6:35). We can delight in a rainbow, because it reminds us of God's covenant of protection (Genesis 9:12-17). The physical things do not become any less marvelous; if anything, they become more so.

The good news is, we don't have to make an absolute choice of spiritual over carnal. God knows we live in a physical world for now, and that we have physical requirements while we are here. So He commits Himself to our care here as well as in eternity. Jesus says in Matthew 6:33, "But seek first His kingdom and His righteousness, and all these things will be added to you." Like Israel of old gave the firstfruits of the harvest to the Lord, we give Him the firstfruits of our affections. We believe He will amply provide us with all that we need if we will only agree to make His will for our lives our foremost desire.

It is tragic that so many people in the world see a choice for God as a choice against happiness. Christians see it as exactly the opposite. Yes, He asks us to refrain from certain things that many in the world love dearly. And He asks us to partake of things that they find distasteful, or even hateful. That's why Peter writes, "In all this, they are surprised that you do not run with them into the same excesses of dissipation, and they malign you" (1 Peter 4:4).

But that does not deter us. We have found something better, even if our neighbors do not appreciate or value it. We have chosen to heed the words of David in Psalm 37:4-6—"Delight yourself in the Lord; and He will give you the desires of your heart. Commit your way to the Lord, trust also in Him, and He will do it. He will bring forth your righteousness as the light and your judgment as the noonday."

DISCUSSION

1. How would you respond to Adam? _____
   _____
   _____

2. How would you respond to Brooke? _____
   _____
   _____

3. How would you respond to Clyde? _____
   _____
   _____

 **LESSON 6**

Prejudice is an ugly thing. It must be galling when someone is denied a room for the night simply because of his ethnicity. It's not right. It's not fair. It's certainly not convenient. "How typical of the Samaritans to behave hatefully toward us," James and John must have thought. "We were silly to have expected anything more noble than that out of people like that." The irony, no doubt, escaped them.

It was not a single slight that pushed them over the edge. The Samaritans were a cultural offshoot of the Israelite nation that had hardly any of Jacob's blood and even less of his faith. For centuries they had served God when it was convenient (in their own perverted way) and rejected Him when it was not. So Jewish contempt for Samaritans was well grounded in spiritual reality. And naturally, the animosity the Jews had for the Samaritans was returned in kind. "Help Jews on their way to Jerusalem, so they can worship in their temple and ridicule us for how we worship in ours? Not likely!" So James, John, and the rest of the Galileans, as had been the case so often in their lives, would have to go miles out of their way, on foot, to give service to their God.

A lifetime of resentment for this sort of treatment finally reached the boiling point for the brothers. Luke 9:54 records that they asked, "Lord, do You want us to command fire to come down from heaven and consume them?" Finally they were in position to mete out justice for the slights against them and their kinsmen, and they were eager to do so.

I can't help wondering if Jesus thought to Himself, "And they wonder why I call them Boanerges."

Jesus thought destroying an entire culture with holy fire was an overreaction under the circumstances. He preferred to exercise patience. Perhaps he remembered the encouragement He had received from a Samaritan woman in Sychar, as recorded in John 4. Perhaps He saw potential in these obstinate ones that the "Sons of Thunder" could not. Perhaps it is no accident that the hero in the story Jesus tells in the very next chapter in Luke is a Samaritan. In any case, Jesus chose to give these Samaritans another chance.

Personally, I'm glad Jesus is in charge of grace and not James and John. How about you?

Where we start

Children are impatient. A hungry infant cries until she gets fed. A bored infant cries until she is amused. A teenager who has lost "the love of her life" cries until the next "love of her life" comes along. They have immediate issues, and they demand immediate relief. The job of parents is to help the children through the process. At first this is done by giving them exactly what they want as quickly as possible; then gradually, as they grow older and more experienced in life, parents help them understand the disappointments of life, the value of trials, and the opportunities for growth that come in adversity.

Adam says:

The preacher said I would walk in newness of life when I accepted Jesus and was baptized. But my "new life" looks a lot like my old life. I still sin. I still struggle with the same temptations. When will it start getting easier?

Spiritual children are the same way. They see people doing the wrong thing, and they expect them to change. If the wrongdoers don't change, the assumption is they either cannot or will not change, ever. This is generally interpreted as arrogance, intolerance and self-righteousness, and sometimes it is. But sometimes it's just that a Christian hasn't learned to be patient with his neighbor.

Impatience in young Christians is not just focused outwardly. They can easily become impatient with themselves as well. Old sinful habits die hard. Years and even decades of toil in Satan's kingdom are not erased from history, or from one's memory, when one is baptized. So when the well-intentioned Christian detects signs of recidivism, he may panic. He may despair of ever becoming as strong as his spiritual mentors.

The solution to both sorts of impatience—with others and with self—is to remember the patience of God. "The Lord is...patient toward you, not wishing for any to perish but for all to come to repentance" (2 Peter 3:9). He showed patience when He allowed us time and opportunity to come to Jesus in the first place. He continues to show patience when He forgives us our forays into darkness while walking in the light (1 John 1:7). This is not to excuse sin at all; any sin, committed by anyone, is an affront to God and must be dealt with. But God does

---

CONSTRUCTION ZONE — PRAYER

Heavenly Father,

This life is full of trouble and hardship. I thank You and praise You for the life that is waiting for me after this one is over. You cannot lie, and you have promised to save Your faithful ones in heaven. So as wonderful as many of the things here on earth are, my true hope is to leave it one day to be with You and the saved ones of all the ages.

Help me to stop _____

Help me to keep _____

Help me to want _____

Thank You for listening.

In Jesus' name,
Amen.

not send us to the gallows for every offense. "All unrighteousness is sin, and there is a sin not leading to death" (1 John 5:17). We should not be eager to send others, or ourselves, to the gallows either.

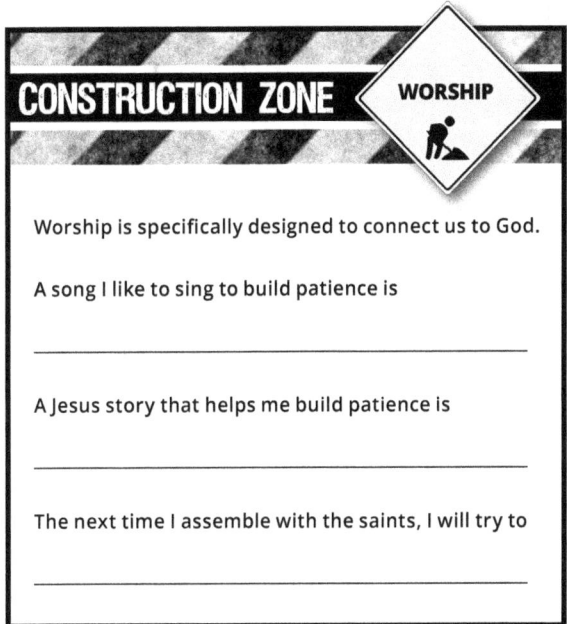

CONSTRUCTION ZONE — WORSHIP

Worship is specifically designed to connect us to God.

A song I like to sing to build patience is

_____

A Jesus story that helps me build patience is

_____

The next time I assemble with the saints, I will try to

_____

How we grow

"Lord, give me patience—and hurry up about it!" We've all heard the jokes. Most of us have told the jokes. We know how important patience is. But often it seems God responds to our prayers for patience by giving us more and more opportunities to be more and more patient. Not exactly what we had in mind.

But that's how it works. Aggravation isn't a headache, and patience isn't an aspirin. The only way we can become patient is through adversity. Jesus warns us that hard times await all Christians—despite our devotion to Him, sometimes even because of it: "Blessed are those who have been persecuted for the sake of righteousness, for theirs is the kingdom of heaven. Blessed are you when people insult you and persecute you, and falsely say all kinds of evil against you because of Me. Rejoice and be glad, for your reward in heaven is great; for in the same way they persecuted the prophets who were before you" (Matthew 5:10-12). Unfair treatment is the rule for the people of God, not the exception. Paul assures us we will not be an exception, either. "Indeed, all who desire to live godly in Christ Jesus will be persecuted" (2 Timothy 3:12). So as hardships abound, we must find a way to make our faith abound even more.

Brooke says:

Friends of my parents are always patting me on the head and telling me how much I've grown. If I've grown so much, why does everyone treat me like a baby? I can do a lot more than they think, both for the family and for the Lord.

Particularly for strong, devout Christians, it can be challenging to wait for those whose enthusiasm seems to be less than it should be. We do not make excuses for lackadaisical service in others any more than we do for ourselves; however, we accept the reality that others will not grow at the same rate as we do. Some will mature more quickly, some more slowly. That is why Paul tells the young preacher Timothy to "reprove, rebuke, exhort, with great patience and instruction" (2 Timothy 4:2). Some will resist the will of God. But we cannot afford to allow their faith problem to become our patience problem.

Whether the rebellious soul is lost in the kingdom of darkness or is struggling with compliance in the kingdom of Christ, Paul's encouragement in 2 Timothy 2:24-26 applies: "The Lord's bond-servant must not be quarrelsome, but be kind to all, able to teach, patient when wronged, with gentleness correcting those who are in opposition, if perhaps God may grant them repentance leading to the knowledge of the truth, and they may come to their senses and escape from the snare of the devil, having been held captive by him to do his will." It grieves us that souls seem so determined to be lost. But we can do them no good by losing patience with them. And we very well may do harm to ourselves if we allow resentment to grow, if we lose control of our tempers and tongues, if we lose confidence in "the pure milk of the word" (1 Peter 2:2) to provide the spiritual nutrition a dying soul needs.

Waiting for others to "grow up in all aspects into Him who is the head, even Christ" (Ephesians 4:15) is sometimes a long, drawn-out process. But "love is patient" (1 Corinthians 13:4). Love for our fellow man should compel us to endure some unreasonable measures if it means providing a smoother pathway for him to reach the Savior.

The "finished" product

"Consider it all joy, my brethren, when you encounter various trials, knowing that the testing of your faith produces endurance. And let endurance have its perfect result, so that you may be perfect and complete, lacking in nothing" (James 1:2-4). Clearly, according to James, we will not become what God wants us to be without encountering adversity. And adversity, by definition, is not a pleasant thing—"for man is born for trouble, as sparks fly upward" (Job 5:7). Sometimes we feel like that piece of metal that, after somehow escaping the intense heat of the forge, is placed on the anvil and pounded incessantly with a hammer. We've been there, done that, gotten the scars. But, like the piece of metal in the hands of the blacksmith, we cannot become what God wants us to be without going through the process. This is how we show God what we are made of.

CONSTRUCTION ZONE — EVANGELISM

The book of Acts describes one soul after another coming to Jesus upon his or her first hearing of the gospel. The Jews at Pentecost (Acts 2:37). The Ethiopian eunuch (Acts 8:35-38). Cornelius and his household (Acts 10:30-48). On and on we could go. "The power of God for salvation" (Romans 1:16) is power indeed.

But repentance does not always come immediately upon exposure to the truth. And transformation never does. Paul does not tell unbelievers to be "transformed by the renewing of your mind" in Romans 12:2; he is writing to Christians, many of whom no doubt have served the Lord for years, and who are still struggling to bring their lives in conformity with His will.

We should not be discouraged if initial efforts to reach our friends and neighbors appear to be going for naught. Paul had been exposed to the gospel for years with absolutely no positive result, but eventually he tired of kicking against the goads (Acts 26:14). Such may very well be the case with someone who is chafing at the notion of the Lord's yoke even today.

"Let us not lose heart in doing good" (Galatians 6:9). Keep on planting the seed. Let it do its work.

A similar metaphor, that of the refiner's smelter, is used repeatedly in the prophets to describe the purification process for the people of God. Malachi 3:1-3 describes the coming of John the Baptist and the Christ who would follow him, and the effect it would have on rebellious Israel: "Behold, I am going to send My messenger, and he will clear the way before Me. And he Lord, whom you seek, will suddenly come to His temple; and the messenger of the covenant, in whom you delight, behold, he is coming," says the Lord of hosts. "but who can endure the day of His coming? And who can stand when he appears? For He is like a refiner's fire and like fullers' soap. He will sit as a smelter and purifier of silver; and He will purify the sons of Levi and refine them like gold and silver, so that they may present to the Lord offerings in righteousness." The unpleasant fact is, we are not good enough for the Lord. Not yet. But God is working on that, slowly but surely.

Clyde says:

I spend every morning reading the obituaries. It's getting to be more the rule than the exception to find a familiar name there. I miss my loved ones. I'm ready to go. How much longer does the Lord expect me to wait for Him?

Paul says in 1 Corinthians 3:12-13, "Now if any man builds on the foundation with gold, silver, precious stones, wood, hay, straw, each man's work will become evident; for the day will show it because it is to be revealed with fire, and the fire itself will test the quality of each man's work." Each of us wants to be a temple to the Lord (1 Corinthians 6:19). And we want to be as precious and beautiful as our calling requires. So instead of looking at God's smelter as a hardship, we should look at it as a proving ground, an opportunity to prove our worth. It may look temporarily like the ordeal is pointless or even counterproductive. But the Divine Blacksmith knows what He is doing. And if we are truly "the right stuff," it will be revealed in time.

And when that time comes, our patience will be rewarded. It is not our job to set a timetable for the Lord; our job is to do His work while He continues to give us time to do it (John 9:4), however much or little time that may be. So, whether with regard to comfort in this life or deliverance from it, we say with David in Psalm 27:14, "Wait for the Lord; be strong and let your heart take courage; yes, wait for the Lord."

DISCUSSION

1. How would you respond to Adam? _____
   _____
   _____

2. How would you respond to Brooke? _____
   _____
   _____

3. How would you respond to Clyde? _____
   _____
   _____

LESSON 7

BUILDING WALLS

Say you are in a room full of people. A room with a small table and a large window. Jesus walks in. He opens the curtains on the window. And through the window you and all of your companions see another room—a room unspeakably ugly, unspeakably terrible, unspeakably horrifying. You are aghast. You could not have imagined that a place so awful could exist.

Then Jesus says every person in the room will have to enter that room. And stay there. Forever. And just when you are beginning to wrap your mind around this, the worst of all possible fates, He lays an ice pick on the table. He says you may escape this fate in one way, and one way alone. You must take the ice pick and use it to gouge out your right eyeball.

And as soon as the words are out of His mouth, there is a mad rush. An absolute stampede. People are pushing, shoving, climbing over one another, absolutely desperate to get to the ice pick.

That is how bad hell is.

We do ourselves and the message of Christ a disservice when we brush off His words in Matthew 5:29-30 as being merely hyperbolic. They are not. They are a very real indicator of the kind of measures Jesus says we should be willing to undergo in our efforts to avoid hell. Lose an eye? Not a problem. Cut off a hand? Which one? Nothing could possibly be too great a cost for what we get in return.

Obviously, abuse of the body is no safeguard against the sins of the heart and mind; Paul says as much in Colossians 2:20-23. Jesus is not telling us how to avoid sin. He is telling us how desperately we should want to avoid it. And if erecting a ridiculously high wall between us and hell is what it takes, we reach for the bricks and mortar.

Adam says:

Sin kills. I get that. So what I need is an alarm that goes off in my head whenever I'm getting too close to the edge. But apparently that's not the way it works. I have to decide on my own how far is too far. And I'm not sure I'm up to it.

We do not draw a chalk line on the ground and trust that the devil will never reach over it and drag us across it.

Where we start

Sin kills. If a smoker doesn't want lung cancer, he should stop smoking. If a dog owner doesn't want his dog to eat off the floor, he should sweep more often. And if a Christian doesn't want to go to hell, he needs to quit sinning. It's just that simple.

Except it's not that simple. Forget for a moment that sin is a hard habit to break under the best of circumstances. Sin sneaks up on us at times. The devil is not always a roaring lion; sometimes he's a wolf in sheep's clothing (Matthew 7:15). Sometimes a situation that is not necessarily sinful can mushroom. It's the standard defense of ordinary, law-abiding citizens who break down in the last ten minutes of your favorite crime drama on television. "I never meant for this to happen. Things got out of control. This isn't me." And yet, "me" is the one getting life in prison without parole.

We need to realize the situations in life are fluid, not static. A "safe" situation today may not be safe tomorrow. Paul writes in Ephesians 5:15-16, "Therefore, be careful how you walk, not as unwise men but as wise, making the most of your time, because the days are evil." The quicker we train ourselves to see sin on the horizon and not just at our doorstep, the better we will be at warding it off when the time comes.

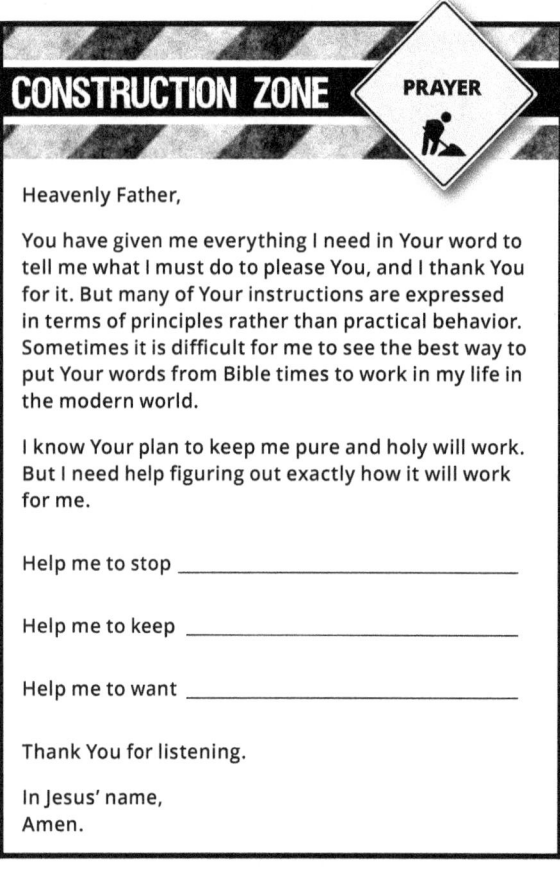

CONSTRUCTION ZONE — PRAYER

Heavenly Father,

You have given me everything I need in Your word to tell me what I must do to please You, and I thank You for it. But many of Your instructions are expressed in terms of principles rather than practical behavior. Sometimes it is difficult for me to see the best way to put Your words from Bible times to work in my life in the modern world.

I know Your plan to keep me pure and holy will work. But I need help figuring out exactly how it will work for me.

Help me to stop _____

Help me to keep _____

Help me to want _____

Thank You for listening.

In Jesus' name,
Amen.

And that's vital, because sin invariably leads to more sin. Satan is not satisfied with simply establishing a foothold in our heart; he wants more and more. Rationalizing sin in one aspect of our life creates a precedent. Before long, we have rationalized sin in two or three more areas. It's tough enough to stop the leaks in a boat without taking an ax to the hull repeatedly. King David is the star witness in this crime drama. He looked. Then he lusted. Then he acted. Then he lied. Then he murdered. Sin begets sin. And often, as was the case with David, consequences beget consequences.

Consider also the fact that our sinful habits become increasingly difficult to escape as we ensconce ourselves further in them. Not everyone can turn on a dime when a brave soul tells us, "You are the man!" Far too often, repeated sin becomes an entrenched sinful lifestyle. Excuses are made. Rationalizations are offered. Lies are told. Friendships are ruined. And ultimately, souls are lost.

Brooke says:

My parents say to stay away from this, stay away from that. But when they start talking about slippery slopes, it seems like they are just inventing reasons to keep me from doing what I want. Lots of times, I just don't see the harm.

The best way to deal with sinful habits is to not engage in sinful behavior in the first place. Good decisions made along the way make it easier to make good decisions in a time of crisis. We avoid becoming alcoholics by avoiding alcohol. We avoid alcohol by avoiding bar scenes. We avoid bar scenes by choosing good friends. Good decisions pave the way for more good decisions and help keep us away from opportunities to make bad decisions.

The Bible may not address every specific circumstance in life, but it maps out a general course of behavior that is specific enough for us to find ground that we know is safe. So we stake ourselves to the safe ground and build walls to keep us from getting into trouble. We draw specific lines that we will not cross, even if others do, even if other Christians do. And then we defend the ground we have claimed. Perhaps we could drift a bit and still be safe. But why would we? We would rather stay where we are and be certain.

How we grow

The gospel is a seed. Jesus plants it in our heart. Then we have a choice as to what sort of growth environment we will provide of it. And just because we are open to its work today, that does not mean

CONSTRUCTION ZONE — WORSHIP

Worship is specifically designed to connect us to God.

A song I like to sing to build walls is

_____

A Jesus story that helps me build walls is

_____

The next time I assemble with the saints, I will try to

_____

it will always remain so. The devil is always looking to change the game. The more he clutters the landscape with distractions and diversions, the more opportunity we have to inhibit the work God is trying to accomplish in us.

As Jesus teaches us in the parable of the sower, it is unreasonable to expect our soul to give itself to God's seed and Satan's weeds at the same time: "And the one on whom seed was sown among the thorns, this is the man who hears the word, and the worry of the world and the deceitfulness of wealth choke the word, and it becomes unfruitful" (Matthew 13:22). We must decide which we desire more, and proceed accordingly. That means more than just saying no to sin; that means putting up barriers to keep future sin from ever getting traction.

All efforts to do so, of course, begin with more of what started the process in the first place—the word of God. We emphasize "book, chapter and verse" for a reason. God is the One who defines sin, and the Bible is His form of communication. If it's not condemned in the Bible, it's not condemned. To define sin apart from the Bible is to bind where the Lord has not bound—or to use His terminology from Matthew 15:9, "teaching as doctrines the precepts of men."

Unfortunately, this mentality can lead to a permissive attitude toward certain specific behaviors that are not emphasized, or perhaps not even mentioned, in the Bible—"It's OK to go dancing as long as it doesn't result in sex," or, "It's OK to drink as long as I don't get drunk," or, "It's OK to go to the public pool as long as I am properly covered up myself." Obviously the Bible cannot possibly address every specific circumstance that may come up, particularly as technology advances and customs change. Most of the Bible's directives are focused on our attitudes—why we do what we do, whatever the circumstances. The trouble is, we tend to judge ourselves on a curve in such matters. A big, big curve.

The solution is to stop thinking so much in terms of right and wrong, and more in terms of good and bad. I can search the Bible through to find concrete proof that searching the internet for pornography is sinful, find no "book, chapter and verse" that says so, and give myself the authorization to click away. But that attitude and behavior takes me further away from God, not closer to Him. And I know that. Even if I convince myself it is not "sinful," I still know it is wrong because anything that separates me from God is wrong.

Replacing the "right vs. wrong" paradigm with a "good vs. bad" paradigm simplifies our situation greatly. It's not so much a matter of whether God is required by the letter

CONSTRUCTION ZONE — EVANGELISM

Jesus associated with sinners. He talked to a woman in Sychar with a checkered history and a sordid present. He stood up for a woman who had been caught in the actual act of adultery. He welcomed as apostles one man (Matthew) who was in the most wretched legal profession in Galilee, and another (Simon) whose surname, Zelotes, indicates he was a known terrorist.

Jesus did not, however, condone sin. At no time did He turn the other way in the presence of immorality or ungodliness. He required sinful people to change—"From now on sin no more" (John 8:11).

The nature of evangelism dictates that we must keep company at some level with sinners—how else would we be able to teach them? God does not want us to go out of the world in our retreat from sin (1 Corinthians 5:9-10). But He does want us to retreat.

It can be a difficult line to walk. Love for sinners compels us to get involved in their lives. But we cannot afford to reject Paul's mandate that we "come out from their midst and be separate" (2 Corinthians 6:17). Yes, we embrace sinners fully and enthusiastically. But we cannot give them the impression that we embrace their sin.

of the law to send me to hell for doing this or that; it's a matter of me finding the best way to glorify God in my life. The longer we live lives of service to the Master, the more we grow in our understanding of what is good and what is bad—or at least we should. When we are fully devoted to doing what is good and avoiding what is bad, and we inform that process by constantly studying His word with a view to application, right and wrong wind up taking care of themselves.

The "finished" product

It is difficult to accept the idea that Christians who are every bit as motivated to serve the Lord as we might put up their protective walls in different places than we do—sometimes more lenient, sometimes more stringent. Most of us hold strong opinions regarding issues ranging from child-rearing to proper clothing to how many children an elder should have—and we hold them tightly. We defend our principles with Scripture. We fret that what we see as permissiveness in others will lead to sin, or that what we see as intrusiveness borders on Pharisaical legalism. All would be so much simpler, we think to ourselves, if people would just see things the way we see them.

Clyde says:

The hard and fast rules I used to make for myself, and for others, don't seem quite as obvious as they did when I was younger. Lots of good people disagree with me. Are things really as black and white as I used to think?

But they don't. And by and large, they won't. Different Christians will decide for themselves how short is too short, how relaxed is too relaxed, how vulgar is too vulgar, how far is too far. And if we do not have specific Bible authority requiring us to place the wall precisely where we have placed it, we cannot require others to walk in lock step with us. It may be that their situation is different from ours, calling for different judgment. It may be that we do not fully appreciate their situation. It's even possible that we are wrong, that we would act exactly the same way in identical circumstances.

The key is to remember the difference between the walls we build for ourselves and the walls God builds for us. If I decide I am going to keep my mind focused on pure things by avoiding R-rated movies, that's a decision I have made for myself. Someone else may decide to avoid PG-13 movies as well. Another may decide certain R-rated films are OK for adults but not children. But none of these lines is drawn by God, and therefore they cannot be bound on others by us. I may feel that my brother errs by exposing himself to sexuality; he may feel the same about me because I hear too much crude language. Ultimately, we are brothers and sisters in Christ, led by the same gospel, serving the same Lord. We may feel strongly enough in our opinions to voice them, even to voice them strongly. But we do not forget Paul's words in Romans 14:12 "So then each one of us will give an account of himself to God."

DISCUSSION

1. How would you respond to Adam? _____
   _____
   _____

2. How would you respond to Brooke? _____
   _____
   _____

3. How would you respond to Clyde? _____
   _____
   _____

LESSON 8

BUILDING ENTHUSIASM

What a scene it must have been. Messianic hopes were at an all-time high. Three straight Passover celebrations had featured high-profile encounters between the rulers of the Jews and Jesus of Nazareth, building expectations throughout the land that He might actually be the fulfillment of prophecy, the bringer of the kingdom of heaven.

And then, suddenly, there He was. Even His humble appearance, riding on the colt of a donkey, connected Him with prophecy (Zechariah 9:9). And when the cloud of dust from the unpaved road became too objectionable for a royal parade, the people paved it with palm branches and even their own clothing. They did not want anything interfering with the glory of His arrival or their view of it.

Some people thought it was inappropriate. Too much emotionalism. Too big a production. Of course, those critics had an undisguised agenda of their own; they were the ones whose hypocrisy Jesus had exposed time after time—and as it happened, He was saving the biggest sorties against them for last.

Jesus refused to play the role of wet blanket as the Pharisees requested. Instead He said in Luke 19:40, "I tell you, if these became silent, the stones would cry out!" The acknowledgement of Jesus as Lord was the natural, inevitable conclusion for anyone who was paying attention. And enthusiasm was the natural, inevitable result of that conclusion.

The enthusiasm didn't die easily, either. Throughout the week, His enemies continually poked and prodded, trying to find a legitimate charge to bring against Him—all for naught; "for all the people were hanging on to every word He said" (Luke 19:48). It was only when the people's dreams of military and political triumph were dashed in Pilate's court and at the cross that the enthusiasm waned. But seven short weeks afterward, when the Spirit through Peter and the apostles proclaimed that Jesus had triumphed after all, the fervor came back all in a rush.

The world has never recovered.

Where we start

Your first bicycle. Your first kiss. Your first job. Your first child. There's something magical about breaking the ice. That's not to say the first time was any better than the second or third time. It's just different. It's special. It creates special memories that cannot be duplicated. Your first day as a Christian is the same way. You have beaten the devil. You are on the path to glory. Your body tingles with energy as you take your first steps down the pathway of righteousness.

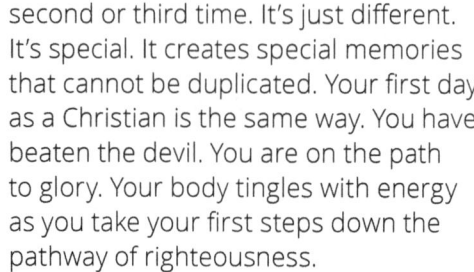

Adam says:

The first few days of being a Christian were amazing. All my new brethren were incredibly supportive. I wanted to tell everyone about what Jesus has done for me. I thought that feeling would last forever. What happened?

But we do not come to Jesus for the tingles—or at least, we shouldn't. Tingles can come from anywhere. Yes, we love being excited about Jesus. But if Jesus just wanted to get us excited, He would have made us all mountain climbers, or astronauts, or fighter pilots. But He didn't. And, as most middle-aged Christians will attest, that's a good thing.

The problem is, we often fail to understand the tingles for what they are—a byproduct of our new relationship with Jesus Christ. We feel excited because we are in Jesus, not the other way around. We grew weary with the burden of sin, and Jesus offered to take it from us (Matthew 11:28). And when we accepted His offer of grace, we felt exhilarated. As well we should have.

But soon we become accustomed to our new life. It becomes something familiar instead of something new. The tingles start to fade. But it's not because our relationship with the Lord has worsened—exactly the opposite is true. We feel so comfortable wearing Him (Galatians 3:27) that He feels natural, familiar. Not tingly.

Then the day comes when we miss the tingles. We crave the excitement that we found in those early weeks with the Lord. And if we are not careful, we will be so determined

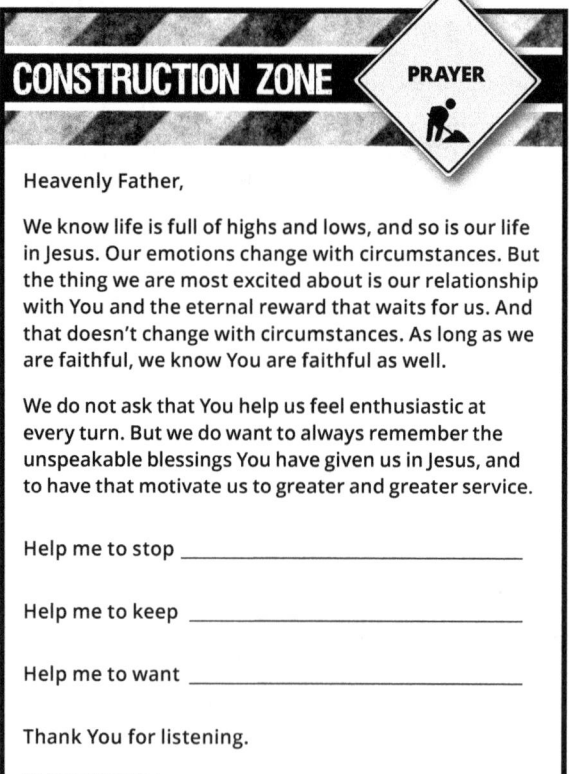

CONSTRUCTION ZONE — **PRAYER**

Heavenly Father,

We know life is full of highs and lows, and so is our life in Jesus. Our emotions change with circumstances. But the thing we are most excited about is our relationship with You and the eternal reward that waits for us. And that doesn't change with circumstances. As long as we are faithful, we know You are faithful as well.

We do not ask that You help us feel enthusiastic at every turn. But we do want to always remember the unspeakable blessings You have given us in Jesus, and to have that motivate us to greater and greater service.

Help me to stop _____

Help me to keep _____

Help me to want _____

Thank You for listening.

In Jesus' name,
Amen.

to recreate the symptoms of our conversion that we abandon our conversion itself. In quest of tingles, we leave the Lord who gave us the tingles in the first place.

Excitement in the Lord is a good thing. We just need to put it in its place. Dessert may be the most memorable part of dinner, but it is not the most important part.

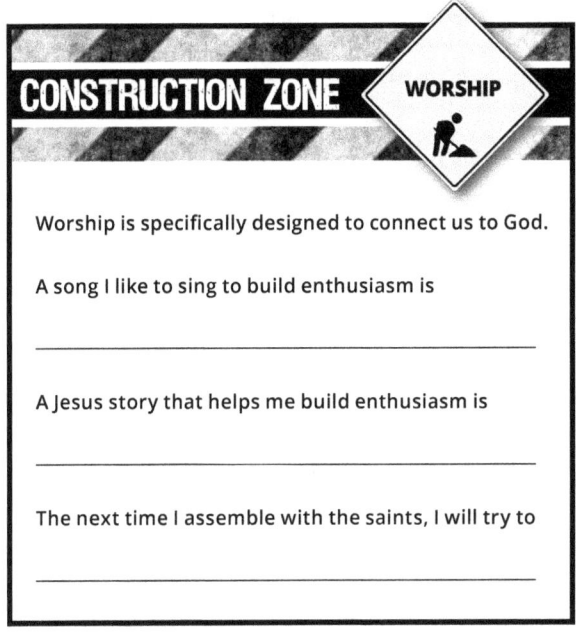

CONSTRUCTION ZONE — WORSHIP

Worship is specifically designed to connect us to God.

A song I like to sing to build enthusiasm is

_____

A Jesus story that helps me build enthusiasm is

_____

The next time I assemble with the saints, I will try to

_____

How we grow

Believe it or not, Jesus warns us about growing too fast. One of the soils described in the parable of the sower is rich in nutrition but lacking in depth of soil (Mark 4:16-17). A layer of rock just beneath the surface keeps the young plant from growing a proper root structure. So, lacking opportunity to grow downward, it grows upward. It appears to be the healthiest plant in the field. But little is going on beneath the surface, where growth is needed the most. And long before harvest time, it runs out of energy. Without roots, the harsh wind blows it over. The periods of drought leave it parched. Despite its early signs of success, it never becomes what the sower intended for it to be.

Appearances can be deceiving. We have all known new converts who seemed ready to set the world on fire for Jesus, when as it turned out, they were just ready to set the world on fire for something. They weren't rooted in the Lord. And when excitement for the Lord waned, they moved on to become excited about yoga, or political theory, or Tony Robbins.

Brooke says:

The Bible is full of stories about people doing exciting things—walking on water, healing the sick, casting out demons. It must have been amazing to be a child of God back in those days. Sometimes I wish I had lived back then instead.

Enthusiasm is no substitute for commitment. Feeling good about Jesus is not the same as being connected to Jesus. When we forget this, when we think excitement is an end unto itself, we grow discouraged when the thrill of the moment inevitably yields to tranquility. But tranquility is a blessing, not a problem. Paul writes that we should aspire to "a tranquil and quiet life in all godliness and dignity" (1 Timothy 2:2). We may love spending five minutes on a roller coaster, or even five minutes every week. But no sane person would want to live on a roller coaster. You would wear yourself out emotionally.

Trying to live life as an unceasing series of mountaintop experiences is exhausting. Worse, it's self-destructive. If we fail to find what we think we want, we grow discouraged and we move on to something else that may do better—distance running, perhaps, or studying the Kabbalah. If somehow we do manage to pile one emotional high on top of another repeatedly, we wind up burning out from emotional exhaustion. God wants better than that for us. He does not want shallow service. He does not want the spiritual equivalent of a sugar rush. He wants real, Bible-based commitment from people who have consciously decided to spend the rest of their lives in His service.

Do not expect every moment with the Lord to be exhilarating. You will have discouraged times, disappointed times, times when you struggle, times when you fail. That's not good, but that's life. That's real. And that's the time when you find out what kind of Christian you are—the low points, not the high points.

Clyde says:

I love watching teenagers serving in the church. I love watching people get baptized. They all seem so full of life. I used to be like that. It was wonderful. But excitement is for young people. I'm past that now.

Thankfully, though, there are high points. But in those moments, stay grounded. Remember that the real cause for excitement is not your particular circumstance (which will end) but rather your fellowship with God (which will not). Do not confuse foretastes of heaven with heaven itself.

The "finished" product

God's mercies are new every morning. With each sunrise comes another motivation for us to be active and energetic in His service. And although it is unreasonable, and perhaps even inadvisable, to strive for a constant and thrilling "buzz" in our service to Jesus Christ, we cannot afford to sink into emotionless lethargy either. We need to find a balance.

One way is to minimize the difference in importance that we may assign to various acts of service, whether our own or those of others. We have a natural tendency to get more excited about baptisms and sermons than about prayers and private mentoring. But every work in the Lord's vineyard has significance and therefore merits some degree of enthusiasm. That doesn't mean we want parades held in our honor when we bring a covered dish to a sick family or fill in at the last minute when the church needs a song leader. It means that when we see an opportunity for service in front of us, we greet it with vigor. We are doing something important, however unimportant it may seem to be. And we make time to thank and congratulate others when they engage in "little things" for the Lord as well. The more enthusiastic we are about their effort, the more enthusiastic they will be—and the more likely their effort will be repeated and redoubled.

Another way—artificial perhaps, but still effective—is to choose terminology that communicates joy and energy. If someone asks you in the church foyer how you are doing, say, "Great!" If your head hurts, you're tired from a long night with the children, and you are concerned about your doctor's appointment the next day, say, "Great!" anyway. You are a Christian, after all; what's not "great" about that? It's not a lie; it's a demonstration that the important things in your life are going as well as they possibly could be, and that other, lesser, factors will not take your attention away from that fact. And who knows? If you keep telling other people how wonderful your life is, you may accidentally forget how unhappy you are. And your positive energy in the midst of unfortunate circumstances is sure to impress your brethren and inspire (or shame) them into having a better attitude themselves.

Every day we spend on earth is a day we draw closer to heaven. As Paul writes in Romans 13:11-12, "Do this, knowing the time, that it is already the hour for you to awaken from sleep; for now salvation is nearer to us than when we believed. The night is almost gone, and the day is near. Therefore let us lay aside the deeds of darkness and put on the armor of light." Discouragement and grumpiness works fine for people who are struggling with life and who have no hope of something better. If we share their attitude, it is an indication we also share their lack of faith. If we believe the blessings Jesus gives us here as Christians are in fact "a pledge of our inheritance, with a view to the redemption of God's own possession, to the praise of His glory" (Ephesians 1:14), we should grow ever more enthusiastic about the coming of a new day, regardless of what the previous day brought us. After all, the next day is just that much more likely to be the day we spend with the Lord.

CONSTRUCTION ZONE — EVANGELISM

Have you ever had someone try to convince you to try a particular restaurant, or watch a particular movie, or vacation in a particular destination spot? Did they do it with a smile? Did they give you details? Did they regale you with their personal experiences? Did they tell you how much better off they were for the experience, and how much better off you would be if you shared in it?

If not, you probably thought their experience was less than sublime. And you were considerably less inclined to follow their recommendation.

Why do we expect our invitations to a relationship with Jesus would be any different? If we tell people about the joy we have found in the Lord, about the improvements we have already seen in ourselves, about how their current experience is wholly inadequate, then they might be motivated to see what the fuss is about. But not if we show no enthusiasm for the Lord, if we barely get ourselves to the church building on time, if we are dragged kicking and screaming into any conversation about religious matters. Why would they care? Clearly we don't.

Our neighbors can have mediocre lives without the Lord. Let's make sure that's not what we are offering.

DISCUSSION

1. How would you respond to Adam? _____
   _____
   _____

2. How would you respond to Brooke? _____
   _____
   _____

3. How would you respond to Clyde? _____
   _____
   _____

LESSON 9

BUILDING CONFIDENCE

They went out two by two. But instead of pairs of animals on their way to the security of the ark, these were disciples of Christ, seventy in total, on their way out to the cold, ungodly world. They had no guarantee of success in any measure; in fact, on their way out, the Lord roundly criticized the attitude some of the towns on their route had already taken toward the message He had given them. The Lord's base of operations for His Galilean ministry was as bad as any of them; Jesus says in Luke 10:15, "And you, Capernaum, will not be exalted to heaven, will you? You will be brought down to Hades!"

Beyond that, He sent them out with nothing. Less than nothing, in fact. Not only were they to go out with no money or possessions, they were not even to carry a bag to carry any money or possessions someone might want to give them. Eat what people give you for the work you do, He said. If they don't appreciate you enough to feed you, shake the dust off your feet, and find someone else who does. But keep preaching. Always keep preaching.

Lambs going out in the midst of wolves, he called them. Not exactly the pep talk they might have been looking for.

But if they questioned their commitment, we don't read anything about it in the context of Luke 10. In fact, since Jesus' close disciples did not always have enough faith to cast out demons (Mark 9:17-18), and the seventy did (Luke 10:17-18), it's safe to assume they went out in complete confidence that the Lord's words were true, that their mission was His mission, and that their Heavenly Father would provide for them. And because of their faith, demonic forces fell—which Jesus equated to a defeat of Satan himself. And future victories were assured them as well.

> **Adam says:**
>
> I don't know much about the Bible yet. I'm just getting started. Frankly, I'm scared to death that someone might ask me a question about my faith. I know what I believe, but there's no way I'm ready to explain it to anybody.

Jesus sends us out into the same world they experienced—the same obstacles, the same enemy. And we will be victorious as well, because we, like the seventy, have chosen to open our eyes, ears and heart to His message, and then opened our mouths to share it with others.

Where we start

For some people, "know" is too big a word. They may "think" there is a God; they may "think" the Bible is His word; they may "think" Jesus is His Son; they may "think" they are Christians. But they don't "know." They aren't that confident.

There is no reason a true child of God should live in that kind of doubt. Yes, faith is somewhat insubstantial by its very nature. But that does not mean it is groundless or unreasonable. As Hebrews 11:1 reminds us, "Now faith is the assurance of things hoped for, the conviction of things not seen." It wouldn't be faith if it involved things that appear in our literal vision, that are perceived by our natural senses. But because we have opened our minds to the existence of an intelligence greater than our own, we have come to realize that the world makes far more sense when God is in it than when He is not. God's picture of the unseen reality is far more reasonable, far more believable, than the alternatives presented to us by an unbelieving, faithless world.

Confident in God, we then quickly develop confidence in His word. If God exists, how could He not communicate with His creation? How could He expose us to grand and inescapable concepts such as life and death, past and future, good and evil, and not inform us on these subjects? Beyond that, how could He not inform us of Himself? And given that the Bible does all of these things for us, how could we believe that it would be untruthful? After all, creation was His idea. Communication was His idea. Salvation was His idea. It is preposterous that God would conceive of such things but then inform His creation of them inaccurately or inadequately.

But if God is real, and the Bible is real, then Jesus is every bit as real. That's why His best friend on earth could write, "Therefore many other signs Jesus also performed in the presence of the disciples, which are not written in this book; but these have been written so that you may believe that Jesus is the Christ, the Son of God; and that believing you may have life in His name" (John 20:30-31). Faith comes through exposure to the word of God (Romans 10:17). The more we read, the more we believe. The more we believe, the more we want to read.

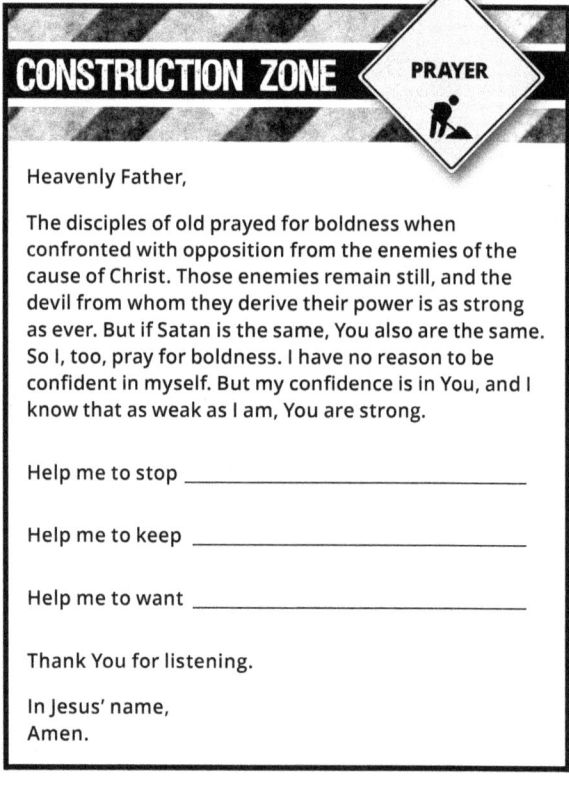

CONSTRUCTION ZONE — PRAYER

Heavenly Father,

The disciples of old prayed for boldness when confronted with opposition from the enemies of the cause of Christ. Those enemies remain still, and the devil from whom they derive their power is as strong as ever. But if Satan is the same, You also are the same. So I, too, pray for boldness. I have no reason to be confident in myself. But my confidence is in You, and I know that as weak as I am, You are strong.

Help me to stop _____

Help me to keep _____

Help me to want _____

Thank You for listening.

In Jesus' name,
Amen.

Paul writes in 2 Timothy 1:12, "I am not ashamed; for I know whom I have believed and I am convinced that He is able to guard what I have entrusted to Him until that day." Not "I think," mind you. "I know." "I am convinced." And if that seems difficult to say sometimes, if your belief seems to come up somewhat short of "knowing," that makes you no worse than the disciples themselves. They knew the Lord better than anyone and yet rejected testimony after testimony of His resurrection; only seeing it for themselves sufficed. That does not have to be the case for us. As the Lord told Thomas, "Because you have seen Me, have you believed? Blessed are they who did not see, and yet believed" (John 20:29).

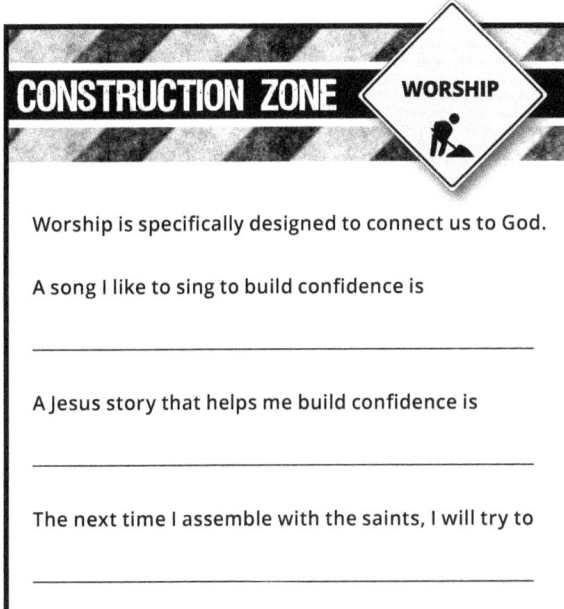

CONSTRUCTION ZONE — WORSHIP

Worship is specifically designed to connect us to God.

A song I like to sing to build confidence is

_____

A Jesus story that helps me build confidence is

_____

The next time I assemble with the saints, I will try to

_____

How we grow

As we acquire more and more experience in the Lord, we also, unfortunately, acquire more and more failures. And although we may (and hopefully do) grow from our experiences and perhaps learn to succeed where in times past we have failed, we come to realize that no matter how hard we try, no matter how long we serve the Lord, we will never quit making mistakes. And that can be extremely discouraging.

The trick to avoiding discouragement and maintaining confidence is realizing that our perfection is not the key; God's perfection is. Although we may be supremely fallible, He is supremely reliable. That is the point the apostle is making in 1 John 3:19-20—"We will know by this that we are of the truth, and will assure our heart before Him in whatever our heart condemns us; for God is greater than our heart and knows all things." I may feel in my heart of hearts that I am the blackest of sinners—as Paul Himself did (1 Timothy 1:15). And I, unlike Paul, may not be able to put the

Brooke says:

I'm the best in my Bible class at reciting the books of the Bible. But actually, I haven't even read most of them. And there are plenty of parts that I have read that I don't understand. Does that mean I am going to hell?

mistakes of my past behind me (Philippians 3:13). But God is greater than my heart. He can forgive me even when I cannot forgive myself. And knowing that, I can find the strength to forgive myself as well. That's what gives us the assurance to which John writes in the next two verses—"Beloved, if our heart does not condemn us, we have confidence before god; and whatever we ask we receive from Him, because we keep his commandments and do the things that are pleasing in His sight."

As John states repeatedly in his first epistle, keeping his commandments is not synonymous with errorless behavior. There are, simply put, children of God and children of the devil. The one group has committed itself to service to its maker; the other has not. When we find ourselves in the first group, we act like Christians, we think like Christians, and we hope like Christians. God is not looking for an excuse to disqualify us and throw us back into the pool of sinners. He loves us too much for that. Just as it is in our character as His children to confess sins when we err (1 John 1:9), it is in His character to forgive.

Certainly we must continue to serve Him as faithfully as possible. That is why John writes, "Now, little children, abide in him, so that when he appears, we may have confidence and not shrink away from Him in shame at His coming" (1 John 2:28). Adam and Eve shrunk away at the Lord's coming (Genesis 3:8). God had given them a commandment, and when His "two-edged sword" lays us open before Him (Hebrews 4:12-13), sometimes it hurts. But although sin separates us from our God (Isaiah 59:2), forgiven sin does not. "Therefore there is now no condemnation for those who are in Christ Jesus" (Romans 8:1). We regret our sins, and we try our best to keep from repeating them. But they do not cause us to question our salvation as long as we are allowing ourselves to be guided, however imperfectly, by His Spirit-given word. As we read in Romans 8:14-16, "For all who are being led by the Spirit of God, these are sons of God....The Spirit Himself testifies with our spirit that we are children of God."

> **Clyde says:**
> I haven't spoken in front of a group of Christians in ages. I don't think I've ever led a home Bible study. We have other Christians who do a much better job with that than I ever could. I'm better on the sidelines.

The "finished" product

Although God does not require perfection, He does require us to pursue it. The longer we live in Christ, the closer we draw to Him and His example. And the closer we draw to Him, the more confident we should grow—not because we are living more perfectly, but because we understand more perfectly about His salvation and our part in it.

Paul's words from 2 Corinthians 1:12-14 ring true: "For our proud confidence is this: the testimony of our conscience, that in holiness and godly sincerity, not in fleshly wisdom but in the grace of God, we have conducted ourselves in the world, and especially toward you. For we write nothing else to you that what you read and understand, and I hope you will understand until the end; just as you also partially did understand us, that we are your reason to be proud as you also are ours, in the day of our Lord Jesus." Paul had conducted himself "with a perfectly good conscience before God" (Acts 23:1). This assured him in his own mind that he had worked with the right attitude. Combine his "clear conscience" (2 Timothy 1:3) with his strict adherence to the "standard of sound words" (2 Timothy 1:13) that informed his conscience, and he could live in full confidence that He was firmly set in the grace of God. The Corinthians could be proud of him and his work, and most of them were. And when they strove for the same confidence in the same way, they made him proud of them as well. This was not arrogance or vanity speaking through Paul; it was utter confidence in the saving blood of Jesus Christ that is applied to all those who obey Him (Hebrews 5:9).

If we are falling from the true faith, certainly we should not have this confidence. But if we "walk in the Light as he Himself is in the Light" (1 John 1:7), if we "keep His commandments and do the things that are pleasing in His sight" (1 John 3:22), then we have no reason to fear. In fact, fear is a clear indication that we either do not have confidence in His saving power or in our adherence to His word. Both cases are serious, but both are eminently fixable.

The author writes in Hebrews 10:35-39, "Therefore, do not throw away your confidence, which has a great reward. For you have need of endurance, so that when you have done the will of God, you may receive what was promised. "For yet in a very little while, He who is coming will come, and will not delay. But My righteous one shall live by faith; and if he shrinks back, My soul has no pleasure in him. But we are not of those who shrink back to destruction, but of those who have faith to the preserving of the soul." God's love is assured. God's grace is assured. God's power is assured. God's word is assured. If we remain devoted to His cause in every aspect of our life, there's no reason for us not to be assured of our salvation in our own hearts as well.

CONSTRUCTION ZONE — EVANGELISM

We read in 1 Peter 4:11, "Whoever speaks, is to do so as one who is speaking the utterances of God." The apostle means that our preaching should not sound like we are just pontificating on our own opinions. The gospel should be easily identified as such, and distinguished from our own surmising and conjecture.

One of the advantages to doing things God's way in this particular circumstance is that it absolves us of any blame when the message is distasteful to the listener. The initial response is always to blame the messenger. Sometimes the reaction gets extreme, as with Stephen in Acts 7:54-60. Usually, thankfully, it stops short of that. But it is often uncomfortable for everyone involved.

The catchall response to pushback is, "That's not me talking, that's God talking." Peter himself used that argument in 2 Peter 1:20-21. The other apostles didn't invent the gospel of Jesus Christ; they said only what God told them to say. We are not to preach any "private interpretation" either. We just preach the gospel we are given. If our hearers don't like that, God says to us as He did to Samuel, "they have not rejected you, but they have rejected Me" (1 Samuel 8:7).

DISCUSSION

1. How would you respond to Adam? _____
   _____
   _____

2. How would you respond to Brooke? _____
   _____
   _____

3. How would you respond to Clyde? _____
   _____
   _____

LESSON 10

BUILDING RELATIONSHIPS

The remarkable statement was a consequence of a remarkable sermon. And the remarkable sermon was itself a consequence of a remarkable insult. Finally (or perhaps we should say initially), the remarkable insult was a consequence of a remarkable action.

First the action. A demon was afflicting a man, making him both blind and mute. Jesus cast out the demon—a spiritual victory that was accompanied by physical consequences, the restoration of the man's powers of sight and speech.

Then the insult. Instead of accepting the obvious and (one would think) undeniable implications of the sign, Jesus' detractors said Jesus was Himself demonic—that it was the devil's power that defeated the power of the devil.

Then the sermon. Instead of contenting Himself with exposing the preposterous argument for what it was, Jesus launched into a larger discussion. Anyone who would go to the extreme of this sort of blasphemy has revealed his true heart. Jesus Himself is good incarnate. Aligning yourself against Him is to align yourself with evil, with the devil himself. Ironically, the same enemies interrupted the sermon with an appeal for a sign—as though they had not just seen one and blasphemously rejected it. And Jesus refused to cater to them, instead choosing to reemphasize the same point. Claiming to be "anti-evil," as these men certainly did, was not enough; the evil must be replaced by good—i.e., by faith in Jesus as Lord. And if this was not accomplished, the "empty of evil" heart will become the most evil heart of all. The hypocritical scribes and Pharisees who were judging Him, and who ultimately would crucify Him, proved that point.

Finally, the statement. When given an opportunity to reconnect with His carnal family, from whom He was at least partially estranged, He said, "Who is my mother and who are My brothers?...For whoever does the will of My Father who is in heaven, he is My brother and sister and mother" (Matthew 12:48-50).

Obviously Jesus loved His physical family. But He valued His spiritual family more. Many of His physical relations rejected His gospel; Mark's telling of this story groups Jesus' family in with those who thought Jesus had "lost His senses" (Mark 3:21). Jesus had a choice—fortify a relationship with His physical family that accomplished little for His heavenly Father, or fortify existing relationships with those who shared His vision

64 Building Relationships

for the kingdom. It was a choice He found easy to make.

It should be easy for us as well, if we are motivated by the same things He was. But far too often, it's not easy. That should tell us something right there.

Where we start

The word used in the New Testament more than any other for Christians—far more, in fact—is "brother." The text calls God our "Father" and us His "children" too many times to count. We are called "the household of God" in 1 Timothy 3:15 and 1 Peter 4:17. We are, in short, a family. Christians are in it, along with the One whom we are encouraged to call Father (Romans 8:15) and the One not ashamed to call us brothers and sisters (Hebrews 2:11). Non-Christians, those who have not named the Name (Acts 22:16), are not in it; they have not yet been added to it (Acts 2:47).

> **CONSTRUCTION ZONE — PRAYER**
>
> Heavenly Father,
>
> I know I am never alone when You are with me. But I thank You so much for giving me a family as well. With brothers and sisters in Christ, I feel even less alone. It gives me courage to see other souls committed to Your glory and to my own spiritual growth. It tells me, as you told Elijah long ago, there are still 7,000 who have not bowed the knee to Baal.
>
> I want to do whatever I can to show my gratitude for my spiritual family, to build it up, and to help it grow.
>
> Help me to stop _____
>
> Help me to keep _____
>
> Help me to want _____
>
> Thank You for listening.
>
> In Jesus' name,
> Amen.

The sooner we learn to appreciate the exclusivity of the people of God, the better. We read in 1 Peter 2:9-10, "But you are a chosen race, a royal priesthood, a holy nation, a people for God's own possession, so that you may proclaim the excellencies of Him who has called you out of darkness into his marvelous light; for you once were not a people, but now you are the people of God; you had not received mercy, but now you have received mercy." Being different from outsiders is what being a Christian is all about. The more different we are, the easier it is for our neighbors still in the world to see the effect Jesus is having on our lives.

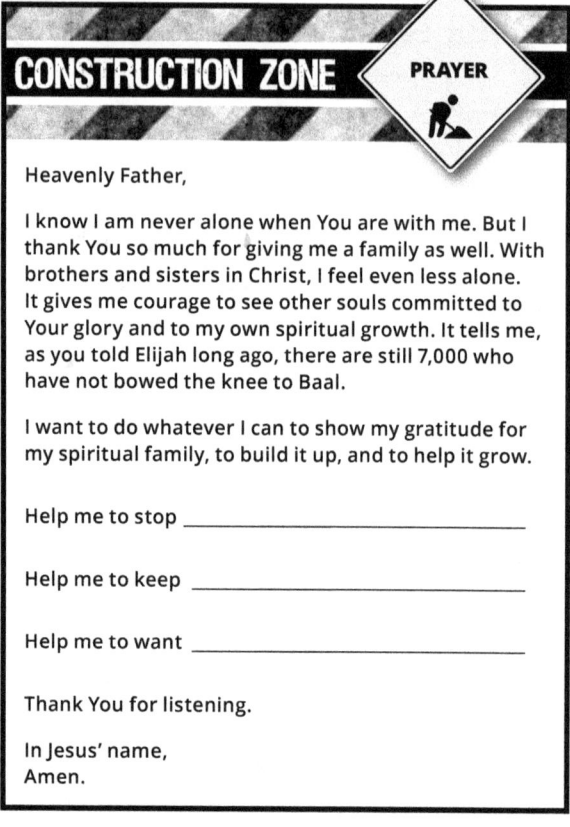

Adam says:

To be honest, I have more in common with my old friends in the world than I do with my new friends in the church. I'm an outsider at church. I don't have their experiences. I don't understand their stories. I just don't fit in.

Inside is light; outside is darkness. Yes, other people may seem religious. They may even seem to confess Jesus. But heaven citizenship (Philippians 3:20)—family membership, if you will—is granted, not claimed. Just as a stranger cannot stumble into your family reunion and claim rights to barbecue and coleslaw, so also one cannot claim to be the son of the Father and yet serve the father of lies (John 8:41-44).

Bearing a general "family resemblance" isn't enough, either. Plenty of our neighbors not only claim fellowship with God but also seem to conduct themselves generally in a righteous manner. But we must remember that our righteous deeds do not save us; the grace of God that is available through Jesus' blood saves us (Ephesians 2:5). Simply going through the motions of saying, "Lord, Lord" (Matthew 7:21) is not enough; He only becomes our Lord when we do what He tells us to do (Luke 6:46). Yes, that includes moral conduct. But anyone can give a sandwich to a hungry person or help an elderly person cross the street. Plenty of people do—including people who claim no allegiance to Jesus whatsoever.

Brooke says:

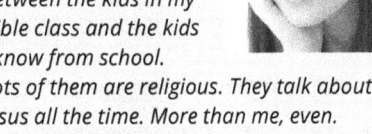

I'm not sure I see that much difference between the kids in my Bible class and the kids I know from school. Lots of them are religious. They talk about Jesus all the time. More than me, even. Aren't they Christians too?

True submission to Christ means accessing His grace in the way He Himself prescribed—faith that leads to baptism (Mark 16:16). Those who knew Him best, who were led by the Spirit He sent to guide them "into all the truth" (John 16:13), taught the same thing. Baptism saves us (1 Peter 3:21). It connects us to Christ (Galatians 3:27). It allows us to access the gift of the Spirit (Acts 2:38). Baptism is certainly not where a relationship with Jesus ends, but it absolutely is where it begins. If a person is a true believer, he will be baptized (Acts 16:31-34). If he went through a form of baptism but it was not what Jesus prescribed, he is to be baptized properly (Acts 19:1-5). If one refuses to comply with the Lord's directions, he may be a decent person or even a religious person, but he is not part of the family. The Father of the family says so.

The connection you share with brothers and sisters in Christ is unlike any other fellowship you will experience in this life. Cherish it. Pursue it. Emphasize it. And if doing so proves to be at the expense of your other relationships, that is absolutely a price worth paying.

How we grow

The problem with being an informed, motivated, prayerful Christian is, you expect all informed, motivated, prayerful Christians to think the same way you think. And they don't. Not by a long shot.

Sometimes that's a judgment error on their part; sometimes it's a judgment error on your part. But it generally comes down to judgment of one sort or another. And

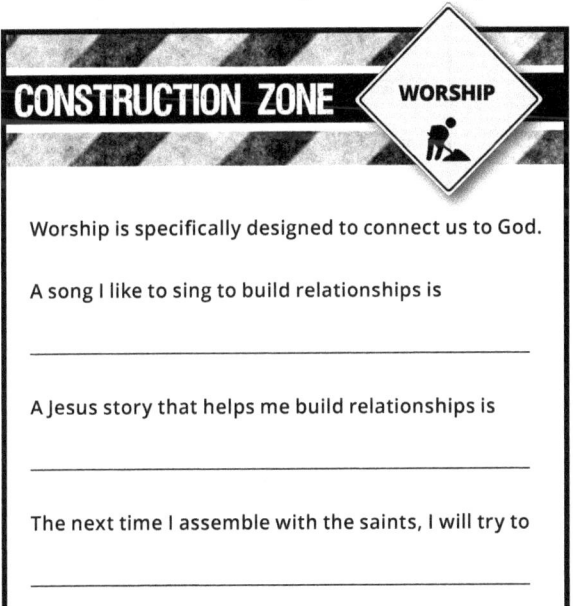

CONSTRUCTION ZONE — WORSHIP

Worship is specifically designed to connect us to God.

A song I like to sing to build relationships is

_____

A Jesus story that helps me build relationships is

_____

The next time I assemble with the saints, I will try to

_____

eventually we come to realize that the "one faith" of Ephesians 4:5 can be fostered in the hearts of two Christians through the application of the same gospel, and yet produce two different opinions on how to put it into practice. The applications in which informed and yet diverse opinions run rampant—from parenting to worship style to elder installation, and a hundred examples in between. And since Christians form their judgments (or at least, they certainly should) from a careful, studious approach to God's word, they can be quite intolerant of someone who has come to a different conclusion. Even, and especially, another Christian.

The key in dealing with differences between brethren is knowing the difference between a firmly held, Bible-backed opinion and an actual edict from God. Immodesty is a sin (1 Timothy 2:9), but two godly people can stand against immodesty and still disagree on where exactly to draw the hemline and neckline. Elders must have "children who believe" (Titus 1:6), but two godly people can disagree on how many children, what percentage of them must believe, and how and for how long their belief must have been demonstrated. The difference between the doctrine and the judgment could not be clearer: one has Biblical authority, the other does not. One must be bound as law, the other must not (Matthew 15:7-9).

Certainly we should feel free, as brethren vitally interested in one another's well-being, to offer constructive criticism when appropriate. And the ones being criticized should receive such advice in the spirit intended—the spirit of love, concern and godly fear. But if the brother or sister decides to take a different path, one that we feel ill-advised but not necessarily in violation of God's will, we should allow them to differ. Perhaps it will wind up being a mistake; perhaps it will even be a tragic one. But the true child of God will grow from his failures as much as from his successes, if not more. And it may even turn out that the "wayward" brother was the one who had the better idea all along; before the story is over, we may be taking advice from him.

> **CONSTRUCTION ZONE — EVANGELISM**
>
> Jesus said, "By this all men will know that you are My disciples, if you have love for one another" (John 13:35). Christians have many defining characteristics, but Jesus chose to single this one out. And it's not difficult to see why. Jesus unites His followers in a fellowship unlike anything else seen on earth—the fellowship we share in our mutual pursuit of the things of God (1 John 1:3). It should not be difficult to see Jesus' love alive and active in us as we interact one with another.
>
> The converse is also true, though. If our relations with brethren are characterized by bitterness, jealousy, pride, and various other vices characteristic of the world and not of Him, the world will be hard-pressed to see a difference between our life in Jesus and their lives outside of Him. They don't need Jesus to be petty and vindictive. They can manage that on their own.
>
> Infighting among brethren is problem enough simply because of the negative impact it has on the people of God. But it also hinders the expansion of the kingdom. We owe it to our neighbors who are lost, as well as to ourselves and our brethren, to be the most loving and harmonious family we possibly can be.

The "finished" product

Whatever differences we may have, whatever similarities we may have, 1 Corinthians 14:26 applies—"Let all things be done for edification." If we are all committed to following Jesus, we will find a way to coexist as the people of God. It will not result in any of us getting our way 100 percent of the time—but then, that's not what we wanted in the first place.

We appreciate and even value the different perspectives that different Christians bring to the table. In many ways it resembles the body analogy Paul uses in 1 Corinthians 12 to describe the varying functions of the Holy Spirit in the lives of Christians. We are different, as verse 18 indicates, "just as He desired." If God had wanted us to be clones of one another, that's how He would have made us. As it is, the slightly different tones of each brother and sister join in a chorus far more deep and rich than a single voice amplified a hundredfold.

Clyde says:

No one is interested in getting to know old people. We bore them. And why not? I bore myself. But that's OK. My life is less complicated when I only have my own problems to worry about. And there are certainly enough of them.

Pursuit of the greater gifts is to be the desire of all, Paul says—particularly the ability to help a brother or sister grow in the gospel. And as chapter 13 so beautifully teaches, brotherly love must undergird all of our efforts. If we have love, we will be motivated to bear all things, believe all things, hope all things, endure all things. The commonality we share in Jesus will overshadow our personal preferences.

In the end, I am personally benefitted in every way. I grow in my own understanding of God's will and my part in it; I encourage my brethren in their own pursuit of Jesus; and I do my part to form a harmonious whole in which we all can continue to spiral upward toward the Lord and toward heaven. As Paul writes in Ephesians 4:15-16, "but speaking the truth in love, we are to grow up in all aspects into Him who is the head, even Christ, from whom the whole body, being fitted and held together by what every joint supplies, according to the proper working of each individual part, causes the growth of the body for the building up of itself in love."

We "grow up" as individuals, and we "grow up" as a body. But "speaking the truth in love" comes first. And don't forget about the "love" part.

DISCUSSION

1. How would you respond to Adam? _____
   _____
   _____

2. How would you respond to Brooke? _____
   _____
   _____

3. How would you respond to Clyde? _____
   _____
   _____

LESSON 11

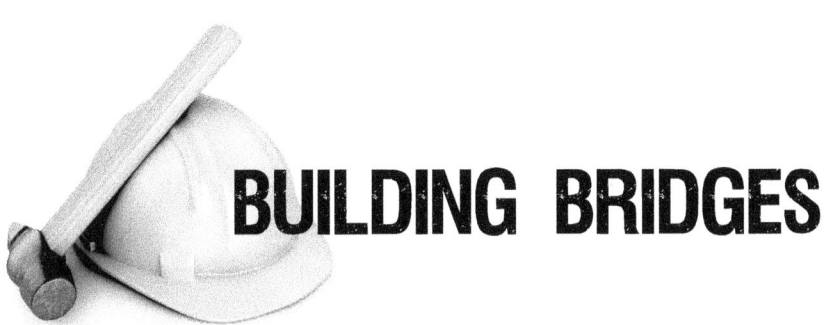

BUILDING BRIDGES

A small group. An early morning. A charcoal fire. It is inconceivable that Peter's thoughts on that day by the lake would not have gone back to a scene just a few days earlier in Jerusalem.

It's not just that he denied having a relationship with Jesus. It's not just that he felt moved to curse and swear in his denials (Mark 14:71). It's not just that he was telling lies to preserve his reputation among strangers while His Master was standing for the truth and being executed for it. No, the basic problem in the high priest's courtyard was much more basic than that.

Peter didn't love the Lord.

If he had loved the Lord, he would have believed the assurances He left before the events of that fateful weekend. He would have trusted that Jesus knew what He was doing, that all would have worked out in the end. But Peter didn't believe him then (Matthew 16:21-23), and he didn't believe Him in the courtyard. If he had loved the Lord, he would have been at His side, testifying for the defense. If he had loved the Lord, he would have been proud to have been associated with Him, not ashamed. Love does not cower in the face of opposition—certainly not in the face of an unarmed, powerless servant girl.

Adam says:

I wasn't the best person in the world before I came to Christ. Now I'm trying to make amends. And I'm meeting with a lot more resistance from my new spiritual family than I expected. Whatever happened to forgiveness?

But Jesus wanted to give Peter a second chance. He was prepared to believe either that the events of that morning were an aberration, not characteristic of the real Peter, or that the events surrounding His arrest, trial, execution and resurrection had wrought a change in Peter for the better—that the love he thought he had for Jesus had been replaced by the real thing.

In any case, Jesus made the first move. As John 21:15-17 records, Jesus looked Peter in the eyes again, like He did from a greater distance across the high priest's courtyard, and, three times, asked him the only question that mattered: "Simon, son of John, do you love Me?"

The next move was up to Peter.

Where we start

We would love to tell new converts that they will never become estranged from brothers and sisters in Christ. After all, we share a fellowship. We share a common commitment to the Lord. If we are all drawing nearer to the Lord, surely we must of necessity be drawing nearer to one another. It's basic geometry.

> **Brooke says:**
> He started it. I was just minding my own business, and he decided he was going to start being mean and ugly. I understand I am supposed to forgive. But he's not sorry. So if he wants to pretend I don't exist, that's fine with me.

Unfortunately, brethren will disappoint. And we, in turn, will disappoint them. Usually both occur at the same time. And then the race is on to determine what share of the blame rests with whom. If we are magnanimous, we may accept "partial" blame for the situation—as long as we are allowed to insist at the end of the discussion that the other person must bear much more. That way we get to appear humble and righteous at the same time.

But this isn't a contest. Or at least, it's not a contest against our brethren. True, it is described in such terms; Paul writes in 1 Corinthians 9:24, "Do you not know that those who run in a race all run, but only one receives the prize? Run in such a way that you may win." But we err greatly when we assume Paul is turning the "good fight" of 1 Timothy 1:18 into a contest between brethren. He is not. He is merely encouraging us to exert ourselves in the Lord's cause with the aim of producing our best effort. "Being glad just to compete" isn't good enough for the Lord's athlete; we strive for excellence in every spiritual endeavor. And that striving is against the devil, not against fellow Christians.

Conflict between brethren is a contest with no winners. We are

---

CONSTRUCTION ZONE — PRAYER

Heavenly Father,

I praise You for Your wisdom in giving us local churches, for allowing us to share with one another as we share with You. But I confess that I have not always been brotherly with my Christian family, and I have been impatient when they have seemed not to be brotherly toward me.

I want to experience the peace that passes understanding in the local church. And I want to help my brothers and sisters in Christ experience it as well.

Help me to stop _____

Help me to keep _____

Help me to want _____

Thank You for listening.

In Jesus' name,
Amen.

constantly exhorted to pursue peace among the people of God. Two bickering sisters in the church in Philippi were told to "live in harmony in the Lord" (Philippians 4:2). The fact that Paul took time to mention them in a letter glowing with positivity indicates how sharp the contention must have been, and how dangerous it was for a church at peace to allow the strife to go unresolved. His "true companion" was exhorted to involve himself if necessary; as he says in 1 Corinthians 6:4-5, there should always be brethren with the reputation for godliness and wisdom who can mediate in such circumstances.

"And the seed whose fruit is righteousness is sown in peace by those who make peace" (James 3:18). Yes, we must occasionally "contend earnestly for the faith" (Jude 3)—even against brethren. But the goal is peace, not victory in war. We must find a way to contend without being contentious.

How we grow

Learning to forgive is one of the most difficult tasks the Lord gives us. And yet it is a task that attaches us to Him in a very special way. We

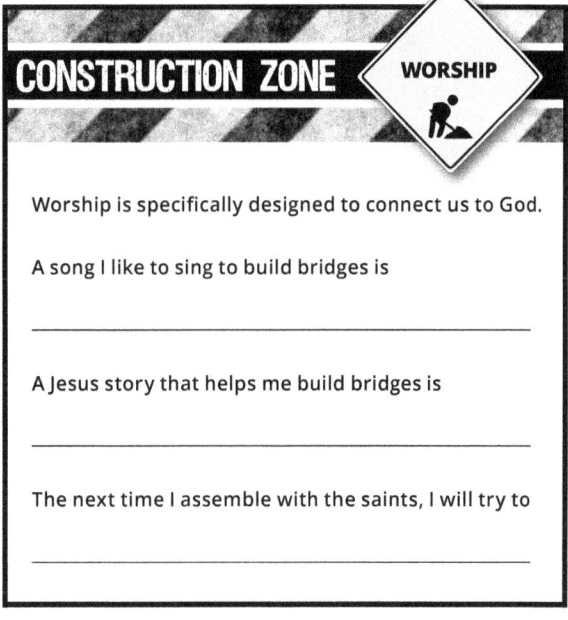

CONSTRUCTION ZONE — WORSHIP

Worship is specifically designed to connect us to God.

A song I like to sing to build bridges is

_____

A Jesus story that helps me build bridges is

_____

The next time I assemble with the saints, I will try to

_____

are told in no uncertain terms that our own forgiveness depends on the attitude of forgiveness we express toward others (Matthew 6:15, 18:35). The more we understand about how much we need God's forgiveness, how He grants it, and how grateful we are to have it, the more inclined we will be to build bridges with our brethren.

God forgives us because we are His children. Yes, in a sense all humans, and indeed all created beings, have their origin in Him. But when we find a relationship with Him through the blood of His Son, we are granted a special bond that others do not enjoy. We have chosen to become His children, not the children of the devil. And as 1 John 3:10 states so clearly, our behavior follows.

Our lifestyle is described in 1 John 1:6-7—"If we say that we have fellowship with Him and yet walk in the darkness, we lie and do not practice the truth; but if we walk in the light as he Himself is in the Light, we have fellowship with one another, and the blood of Jesus His Son cleanses us from all sin." Notice that walking in the light is incompatible with sin, but it still accounts for sin. Occasional missteps can and do occur while walking with Jesus. When this happens, we confess our weakness and we repent. But we do not do that because we are concerned that our Father is disowning us or already has; we do it because it is in the nature of a child of God to do so. Just as is the case in a physical parent-child relationship, the bonds of family are far stronger than an occasional act of inattention or even rebellion. Our unrighteousness is still sin in the eyes of God, but as 1 John 5:17 tells us, this sin does not lead to death. This is the blessing of forgiveness we enjoy as Christians.

But the one who has an unloving attitude toward his brother in Christ is an example of the world, not of the people of God. "The one who says he is in the Light and yet hates his brother is in the darkness until now" (1 John 2:9). If we have not gotten to the point in our walk with Christ that we learn to love our brethren, we haven't gotten anywhere. If the gospel touches us at all, if it changes our behavior at all, surely it will at least manifest itself here. Loving the brethren is the defining characteristic of a Christian, according to no less an authority than Jesus Christ Himself (John 13:35). Needless to say, we would do well to pay heed and follow the example that He showed, and that He described in John 15:13—"Greater love has no one than this, that one lay down his life for his friends."

Clyde says:

I have put up with his nonsense for years. He has always been trouble. He always will be trouble. I grew tired of trying to make friends with him a long time ago. It's to the point now where it's all I can do to share a pew with him.

God forgives us because He loves us; He loves us because we are His children; we are His children because we have been born again (John 3:3). And if our forgiveness is patterned after His, the same ladder should work with regard to our relationship with our brethren. We forgive them because we love them; we love them because they are His children, as we are; they are His children because they have been born again. As long as our brethren continue to walk in the light, we will continue to forgive them when they err against us.

"But what if they neglect to apologize?" In such a case, ask yourself what difference it really makes one way or the other. Did they mean harm? Probably not. Did they cause harm? Perhaps, but probably not. If no real damage has been done, then let it go. And I don't mean give them an opportunity to make it right; I mean let it go. Forget about it. Move on. Have you catalogued and specifically apologized for every single thing you did to offend your Father in heaven? Almost certainly not. But He forgives you. Why would you ask more of that from your brother?

The "finished" product

"Born again." That is how Peter describes the "living hope" we have through Jesus' resurrection in 1 Peter 1:3. And who better than Peter to say it? Because Jesus was raised, Peter had a chance to make amends. He had a chance to do it better the second time. He had a chance to atone for the biggest mistake of his life, and he wasn't about to pass it up.

Jesus offers us the same experience of rebirth—not only in our relationship with God, but in our relationships with our brethren. By pursuing God's things in God's way, we become God's people. Our relations with the rest of our spiritual family are not perfect and never will be; sometimes it's our fault, sometimes it's theirs, and it doesn't matter which is closer to the truth. Because we are not fault-finders in Jesus; we are problem-solvers. We are bridge-builders.

Teaching the sinful world sometimes takes the form of teaching sinful brethren. Sometimes this can be even more delicate a process than teaching someone who has never known the truth. Problems with pride and overconfidence—sometimes in the one taught, sometimes in the teacher—can decrease the chances of the seed that was once received in the heart (James 1:21) can be received again.

If the words of Colossians 4:6 apply to our efforts to reach the lost, surely it is that much more important to season our words with salt when speaking to a brother whom we love. Resistance is almost sure to appear, as with anyone else who is being criticized. But when we teach "in a spirit of gentleness" (Galatians 6:1), when we teach as someone who "bears all things, believes all things, hopes all things, endures all things" (1 Corinthians 13:7), we have a much better chance of being heard.

Those who are pure of heart who are simply misinformed, like Apollos (Acts 18:24-28) will require one approach; reprobates, like Simon (Acts 8:18-24), another. In any case, we are saving souls and covering sins (James 5:19-20). God will help us know the one from the other.

If a brother is too fearful, prideful or immature to make the first move, it doesn't matter. Make the first move yourself. And don't do it to prove you are "the bigger man;" do it because it is your privilege to do it, because you value your brother and regret the distance that has grown between the two of you. If you think he will see that as "winning," let him win. What difference does it make? The next time—and yes, there will be a "next time," and you very well may be involved again—perhaps he will have grown from your good example. Perhaps he will be more noble-minded in his thoughts and efforts. You might even get credit for the assist.

The text says nothing of Peter attempting to build a bridge to the Lord. Perhaps he did and the text does not record it; perhaps he did not. In any case, most of us have been in situations where we were so ashamed of our actions we could not even bring ourselves to apologize to the one we hurt. Hopefully in such instances, the wronged party had enough love to start the bridge-building process himself.

That was the love Jesus had for Peter, and the love He had for all of us when He came to earth and went to the cross. That is the love we are to have for one another—the love that does not merely accept efforts at reconciliation but actually initiates them.

Three times Peter denied his love for the Lord. And three times the Lord gave him a chance to affirm it. However extreme the crime committed against you by your brother in Christ, I doubt it was as horrible as Peter's. And yet the Lord forgave him. Perhaps if we bring ourselves to truly forgive a brother's first offense, we might grow to have the love for him we will need if he offends again.

DISCUSSION

1. How would you respond to Adam? _____
   _____
   _____

2. How would you respond to Brooke? _____
   _____
   _____

3. How would you respond to Clyde? _____
   _____
   _____

LESSON 12

BUILDING JOY

The old adage, "It's always darkest just before the dawn," is a lie. There's actually a great deal of light in the predawn hours. The sentiment behind the expression, though, is true; often our times of greatest fear and doubt are banished quickly by the appearance of the greatest joy imaginable.

Both points were relevant as a small group of women approached the tomb of their Master. They counted on the early light to lead them to the right place, hopeful they could find an attendant they could convince to break the seal and remove the stone that blocked the entrance to the tomb. The Sabbath had prevented them from properly preparing His body, and they had come to finish the job.

Funerals are somber events, particularly when the deceased is a close friend. It is reasonable to assume the sorrow the women felt at the cross had not yet diminished. And whatever grief was in their hearts and on their minds at the time was quickly enhanced with shock and dismay when they saw the open tomb. But quickly an angel gave them the reassurance that they needed, telling them a story almost too good to believe—"He is not here, for He has risen, just as He said. Come, see the place where He was lying. Go quickly and tell His disciples that He has risen from the dead; and behold, he is going ahead of you into Galilee, there you will see Him; behold, I have told you" (Matthew 28:5-7). And they hurried away from the scene "with fear and great joy."

For reasons not explained, the Lord did not make them wait until then. He greeted them on the way to see the disciples. The joy, no doubt, was suddenly amplified manifold. And one witness after another of His resurrection experienced the same thing. The Savior lives; how could joy not abound upon hearing that news? And even when He parted ways with them again for the last time in the flesh, the joy did not diminish (Luke 24:52). He had given them a task to accomplish—a great commission. And in keeping it, not only would they be with the Lord here on earth in a spiritual sense, they would be assured of one day being with Him in heaven in a literal sense (John 14:1-3).

The news of great joy that accompanied His arrival (Luke 2:10-11) is the same that accompanied His departure—"a Savior, who is Christ the Lord." And He Himself assures us that this joy is not temporary, that it will characterize us throughout this life and into the next. As He promised His disciples the night before His death, "I will see you again, and your heart will rejoice, and no one will take your joy away from you" (John 16:22). And as surely as they saw the risen Lord a few days later, so also "we will see Him just as He is" (1 John 3:2).

The true hope and confidence of an eternity of joy before the throne of God in heaven—if that's not reason for joy here on earth, I don't know what is.

Adam says:

I know I should be rejoicing always; the Bible says so. But there is so much sorrow and pain in the world. Much of it touches the ones I love. Some of it even touches me. Sometimes I don't feel all that joyful.

Where we start

There's a reason Paul told us in Philippians 4:4, "Rejoice in the Lord always; again I will say, rejoice!" We have a lot to rejoice about when we are "in the Lord." It is "in Christ" where we receive "every spiritual blessing in the heavenly places" (Ephesians 1:3). Because of that, "there is now no condemnation for those who are in Christ Jesus" (Romans 8:1). We "hope in the Lord" (Psalm 31:24). We find strength in the Lord (Ephesians 6:10). Surely our decision to get "into Christ" through baptism (Galatians 3:27) was a wise one.

And since we have so much cause for rejoicing, we are under obligation to do so. A day we choose to not find joy in Jesus is a day we have forgotten about what He has done for us. And our obligation is not just for our own benefit; we owe a debt to our brethren to rejoice as well.

And joy is contagious. We read in 2 Chronicles 30 how Hezekiah's enthusiasm for reestablishing the Passover and the Feast of Unleavened Bread spread quickly to the Levites and to the people as a whole, even to some from the estranged tribes of the Northern Kingdom. The popular support was so great that Hezekiah was moved to extend the festival another week; "so they celebrated the seven days with joy" (2 Chronicles 30:23). Joy begets joy, particularly when we put forth specific effort to make it so (Romans 12:15). We, like the shepherd and woman who have found their lost sheep and coin, instinctively call out to others to share our joy (Luke 15:6,9). The honor

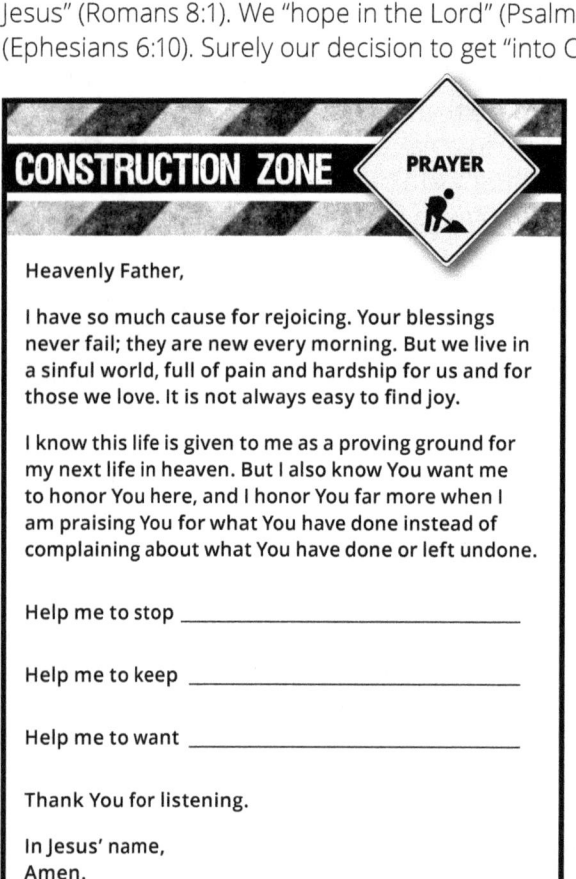

CONSTRUCTION ZONE — PRAYER

Heavenly Father,

I have so much cause for rejoicing. Your blessings never fail; they are new every morning. But we live in a sinful world, full of pain and hardship for us and for those we love. It is not always easy to find joy.

I know this life is given to me as a proving ground for my next life in heaven. But I also know You want me to honor You here, and I honor You far more when I am praising You for what You have done instead of complaining about what You have done or left undone.

Help me to stop _____

Help me to keep _____

Help me to want _____

Thank You for listening.

In Jesus' name,
Amen.

shown to one member of the body is cause for rejoicing in all members (1 Corinthians 12:26).

But Bible "joy" is more than just a happy feeling. It is a feeling of belong, of purpose, a feeling that all is right with the world. It is found in fellowship with brothers and sisters in Christ (2 John 12, 3 John 4), including brethren afar off (1 Thessalonians 3:6). Paul uses the word "joy" seven times in the book of Philippians, all of which have reference to the bonds of fellowship he "enjoyed" with the Christians there. It characterizes our submission to local elders (Hebrews 13:17). It results from the spiritual growth of others (1 John 1:4). It is a testimony of the Holy Spirit's work in the lives of God's people, even when specific circumstances are not ideal (Acts 13:52).

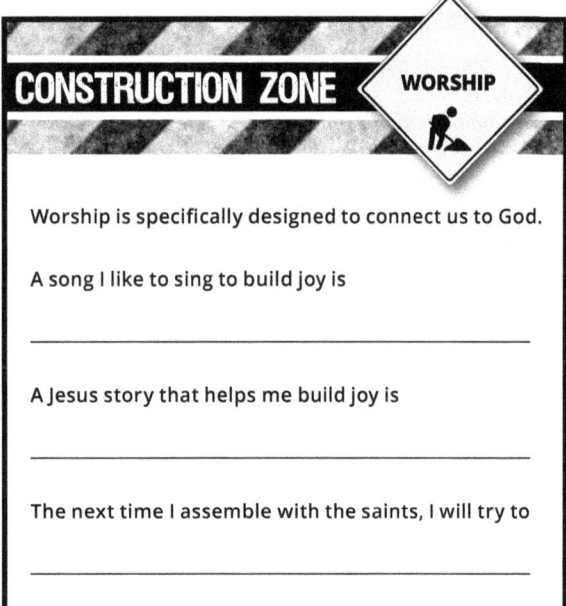

CONSTRUCTION ZONE — WORSHIP

Worship is specifically designed to connect us to God.

A song I like to sing to build joy is

_____

A Jesus story that helps me build joy is

_____

The next time I assemble with the saints, I will try to

_____

The picture of the people of God in Isaiah 61 is magnificent in so many ways—"liberty to captives" (verse 1), "oaks of righteousness (verse 3), "the Lord God will cause righteousness and praise to spring up before all the nations" (verse 11). But perhaps the most inspiring is in verse 7—"everlasting joy will be theirs." There will never cease to be cause for joy among the people of God; so, as Isaiah says in verse 10, "I will rejoice greatly in the Lord, my soul will exult in my God."

It's often said that Christians are the happiest people on earth. We certainly should be; we have far more cause. And if we are not, we have no one to blame but ourselves.

How we grow

Some people wait to rejoice until they have specific cause to do so. Others rejoice until they have specific cause to quit. Our goal as Christians is to get to the point where our joy has nothing whatsoever to do with our circumstances. We are Christians every day; we are blessed as Christians; we rejoice over our blessings; therefore we rejoice every day. And we take that joy with us when we confront circumstances in our lives that may not be ideal; our attitude may not change the circumstances, but they will change our approach to them, and they will affect

Brooke says:

I have a friend who is always smiling. But it's because she won't pay attention to anything she doesn't like. My parents say she is silly and that I should take serious things seriously. Does that mean I can't always be happy?

the impression we leave on bystanders. As Paul writes in 1 Thessalonians 1:6-7 of his beloved brethren there, "You also became imitators of us and of the Lord, having received the word in much tribulation with the joy of the Holy Spirit, so that you became an example to all the believers in Macedonia and in Achaia."

> **Clyde says:**
> I love playing with my grandchildren. I love worshiping with the saints. Joy is not a problem for me in those moments. But what do I do the rest of the time? It may be easy for young people to "sing and be happy," but it's not for me.

We come to realize as Christians that the Lord is more interested in our long-term joy than our short-term joy. As a result, He permits unfortunate circumstances to exist in our lives—and sometimes, it probably seems, to abound. This not because He has abandoned us or does not care about our plight, but rather because He is trying to work some good in us that might not be accomplished any other way. Paul writes in Romans 8:28, "And we know that God causes all things to work together for good to those who love God, to those who are called according to His purpose." This does not mean, as is often stated, that it is "good" that your dog is hit by a car, or you develop a horrible disease, or you lose your job, and that if you don't see the "good" then you are not spiritually minded enough. No, he means God uses the good, bad and indifferent things in our lives to bring us closer to "His purpose"—to help us become stronger Christians, more dependent on Him, more attentive to His goals, more focused on heaven.

That is how we can submit to the requirement of James 1:2—"Consider it all joy, my brethren, when you encounter various trials, knowing that the testing of your faith produces endurance." That is why the psalmist writes in Psalm 126:5-6, "Those who sow in tears shall reap with joyful shouting. He who goes to and fro weeping, carrying his bag of seed, shall indeed come again with a shout of joy, bringing his sheaves with him." The investment we make in our spiritual growth produces all sorts of negative impulses in our lives—

CONSTRUCTION ZONE — EVANGELISM

We share good news. It's instinctive. The shepherds shared their news with everyone they could find (Luke 2:15-20). And when, like the Ethiopian, we go on our way rejoicing after having found the Lord (Acts 8:39), the natural tendency is to tell people what has happened.

The news is not always taken well, though. It grieved Paul that so many of his Jewish friends and neighbors did not receive Jesus Christ. "Brethren, my heart's desire and my prayer to God for them is for their salvation," he writes in Romans 10:1. He had found the hope the Jewish nation had sought all those years (Acts 24:15), and it hurt him that he was not able to share the greatest joy in his life with them. He suffered loss when his work went for naught; he would rather have found even more cause for rejoicing (1 Corinthians 3:14-15).

The man who had been demon-possessed wanted to follow after Jesus, but the Lord would not permit him. Instead, He told him, "Go home to your people and report to them what great things the Lord has done for you, and how He had mercy on you" (Mark 5:19). That is what he did. If the Lord has brought us as much joy as He brought that man, that is what we should do as well.

fatigue, discouragement, resentment, confusion. But we fight through those things, confident in the Lord who has sent us, and in the end we see the marvelous things God has accomplished in us and in the people we have touched.

The "finished" product

It is the child who thinks satisfaction can only be found in the accomplishment of one's own goals, the scratching of one's own itches, the feathering of one's own nest. As we grow, we realize the Lord was right—"It is more blessed to give than to receive" (Acts 20:35). We take more delight in the look on our children's faces when they open a present than we do in opening our own. It is the natural work of maturation.

The same process should be working in us as children of God. Joy comes less and less from what is going on in our immediate vicinity, and more and more from the blessings being showered upon others. This is why Paul wrote in Philippians 2:1-2, "Therefore if there is any encouragement in Christ, if there is any consolation of love, if there is any fellowship of the Spirit, if any affection and compassion, make my joy complete by being of the same mind, maintaining the same love, united in spirit, intent on one purpose." Paul knew of the love the Philippians for him; he counted on it. He knew their hearts went out to him while he was in prison, that they yearned for a way to unburden him somehow. And Paul said they could do exactly that by working harmoniously with one another. His joy was made full in the knowledge that his beloved brethren were pursuing the things of Jesus Christ—and in so doing building an atmosphere of joy themselves in their fellowship.

No one is a greater example of this selflessness than the Lord Himself. Hebrews 12:2 tells us, "Jesus...for the joy set before Him endured the cross, despising the shame." It was not His own pleasure and exaltation that took Jesus to the cross; such pursuits would never have permitted Him to come to earth at all, let alone die. Yet His evident love for us compelled Him to come anyway, knowing the joy of being "the firstborn among many brethren" (Romans 8:29) was worth the price He would have to pay. This is the attitude of Christ Paul requires us to emulate (Philippians 2:4-5).

Paul himself did. That is how he can write in Colossians 1:24, "Now I rejoice in my sufferings for your sake, and in my flesh I do my share on behalf of His body, which is the church, in filling up what is lacking in Christ's afflictions." It is as if he were saying, "Since Jesus Himself isn't here anymore to suffer in the flesh for His people, it is my honor to do it in His place." Exactly how Paul's imprisonment could have helped the brethren in Colossae is unclear, but clearly Paul believed it did—if only in freeing up enough of his time and attention to write them a letter of encouragement.

And there's more good news; if you persist in finding joy in this life, one day you will "enter into the joy of your Lord" (Matthew 25:21). God is only getting started showing you how marvelous it is to be His child. Just wait to see what He has in store for you next!

DISCUSSION

1. How would you respond to Adam? _____
   _____
   _____

2. How would you respond to Brooke? _____
   _____
   _____

3. How would you respond to Clyde? _____
   _____
   _____